Pieces from My Mind

Pieces from My Mind

A True Heartfelt Journey in Black American History

CARL E. CLARK

CREATIVE ARTS BOOK COMPANY
Berkeley • California

Pieces from My Mind is published by Donald S. Ellis and distributed by Creative Arts Book Company

For information contact:
Creative Arts Book Company
833 Bancroft Way
Berkeley, California 94710
1-800-848-7789

ISBN 0-88739-307-1
Library of Congress Catalog Number 99-64938

Printed in Canada

Dedication

I dedicate this book to all the people who are near and dear to me, and to those who I respect for their relationships with me, which have had some effect on my life.

First, my Father, who taught me to be honest and aware of what was happening around me, to think before reacting to those things as appropriate, to be proud and yet considerate of others.

To my beautiful Mother, who left me at an early age, who rocked the cradle of her sons and daughters, at the same time instilling within us compassion and love for all mankind.

To my dedicated wife Florence, my son Karl, and my daughter Karen.

To all those gallant Mess Attendants and Stewards who were part of my Navy Family as I journeyed through my twenty-two years in the US Navy.

To those Brothers who were assigned to the most hazardous stations on Navy ships during World War II.

Acknowledgments

This is the first time I have attempted to write a book.
I wish to thank my son Karl B. Clark for his input, and for helping me accomplish this task.

—Carl E. Clark

Some of the names of individuals in this book have been changed to reduce or eliminate any family embarrassment.

The book's purpose in truth is to provide a means for understanding and thus a path for change.

Table of Contents

The Beginning Pieces

The Final Pieces

Introduction

I write this book fully aware that each of us is unique. Our lives and life experiences are all different. I thank God for my destiny, my fate, or whatever you wish to call the *Guiding Light* that has allowed me to live a full, adventurous, and healthy life for over eighty years.

I was born in the horse and buggy days, when the horse was a necessity and wagons were the main mode of transportation. It is easy for me to recollect the time when there was no radio, certainly no television. The few automobiles and airplanes were a novelty. The country was filled with race hatred. People of color were being lynched so often it was hardly noticed. Prohibition was in place, and the paying public got its alcohol through bootleggers, while poor people of all colors made bathtub gin.

The Great Depression came and people began dying on the streets from hunger and from cold. The hoochy-coochy houses flourished. Jazz and rent parties were commonplace . . . all just part of the scene. People of color could only get the jobs no white person wanted, such as maid, janitor, ditch digger, dishwasher, Pullman porter, and the like.

My father and mother moved our family out of Denver to a small farm they had purchased. Our farm was a short distance from a great prairie where wild horses, rattlesnakes, and prairie dogs still live. I had the good fortune of seeing all those things. Dad and Mom wanted the siblings to grow up in a healthier environment. Dad also knew that out there on his piece of ground he could demand respect and demand he be addressed as Mr. Clark instead of "boy."

Later I joined the US Navy as a mess attendant. That was the only job people of color could hold in the Navy in the 1930s. I was at Pearl Harbor on December 7, 1941. Dorie Miller, a Navy mess attendant on the USS *West Virginia* during the Pearl Harbor attack, was awarded the Navy Cross for his heroism; he was my friend. I fought on combat ships in the South Pacific during World War II and have lived to tell this story concerning the black Navy mess attendants and stewards. I will tell this story as well as I can, knowing the public rarely ever hears the truth about what we black men did on those ships. I consider myself very fortunate to have seen most of the world, and I endeavor to bring my experiences to you. I only wish to tell my story truthfully, *in my own words*.

Mr. Carl E. Clark ST1 in the early Navy Steward Uniform

Preface

Black Americans have been an important part of the US Navy for many years. Before 1928, many black Americans served the Navy in several capacities, working as firemen on the coal-burning ships as well as mess attendants and stewards. In 1928, black Americans were banned from becoming part of the Navy. At that time President Herbert Hoover declared he wanted an all-white Navy. During this period most of the mess attendants and stewards who cared for the officers were Filipino.

As the Philippines came closer to obtaining their independence, the US Navy became unsure of whether it could still rely on Filipinos to care for the officers. By now Franklin Roosevelt was president. It was decided that black men once again would be permitted into the Navy, but only as messmen to serve the officers. The Navy was thoroughly segregated, white sailors from black. Blacks were separated from Filipinos even though they did the same job—shining shoes, making up officers' beds, cleaning their rooms, feeding them their meals, and being abused the same as the blacks.

A young white sailor when enlisting in the Navy was treated with respect. He was offered a twenty-year endowment insurance wherein he received ten thousand dollars when he reached twenty years of service in the Navy. Blacks were not eligible for this. White sailors advanced one rate when they finished boot camp. Blacks did not; sometimes it took them nearly a year to advance that one step. Whites could advance to petty officers, but blacks and Filipinos with seniority only became chief stewards, with no authority over anyone but mess attendants and stewards, no matter how long they were in service. As the Navy saw it, a white sailor seventeen years old was senior to a black or Filipino forty or more years old with twenty years of service behind them.

As a steward advanced in the Navy he learned to bake, cook, butcher, make menus, and supervise the men under him, even though he was paid the same salary as any other sailor. By the time he reached third-class steward he was expected to know all these things and be able to run an officers' mess.

After a steward advanced to chief steward he was expected to be able to run an officers' mess of any size. For example, on an aircraft carrier we had to organize about one hundred and fifty or more men. We needed to know how to buy enough supplies to prepare up to two thousand meals per day, we had to make up twenty-one menus per week, and we were responsible for housing about six hundred officers aboard ship.

In combat, the ship transformed itself into an offensive or defensive mode. The mess attendants and stewards were assigned to battle stations. A few were stationed on guns or damage control above deck, but most were assigned to the ammunition magazines, which in most cases were several decks down in the bowels of the ship. As the men descended into the ship, watertight hatches were closed behind them to prevent the ship from sinking too fast if she were hit. If the ship sank, mostly mess attendants and stewards went down with it. Many of those men were so far below deck they didn't even know when the ships were sinking. In all the stories and news releases, that very fact was never told.

On the *Aaron Ward* I was assigned to damage control during battle, a job that, as the Navy saw it, was one of respect. I was the exception to the rule, putting out fires and rescuing wounded sailors on deck while the rest of those who worked with me disappeared below deck to send ammunition up to the guns on deck.

Pieces from My Mind

pieces 1

My First Recollections

William Thomas Clark and Sara Clark were the parents of Kenneth, Keith, Karl, Katherine, and Korea. Dad and our mother decided to give us names starting with a K. When I joined the Navy my name was put in the records with a C, and no matter how hard I tried they would not change it back to the correct spelling. None of them thought it was important enough to correct, so I am stuck with it until this day.

Even though all five of us had unique lives, I am only going to make an attempt to tell you about myself. I am Carl Edward Clark. I am two years younger than Keith, who is two years younger than our oldest brother, Kenneth. I am two years older than Katherine, who is two years older than Korea, our youngest sister.

I was born July 30, 1916. World War I was raging in Europe. I wonder if I was my dad's deferment; he didn't go to the war. Dr. Justine Ford delivered me at our home on Short Larimer Street in Denver, Colorado. Dr. Ford was a young black woman. She delivered all of us children, except Kenneth. It was quite unusual and rare that there was a young black woman who was a doctor in Denver in 1916, or any place else for that matter. Dr. Ford was not only our mother's doctor, but also her friend.

I seem to be blessed with the ability to recall things that go so far back. It almost scares me. I can remember when I was about one year old crawling around on the floor. I remember when I was put in my high chair and learning to use a spoon. I would sit in my chair and do little things to get attention. I would use my spoon to dump food on my tongue. The grown-ups always commented about this, so I would just do it, then look around to see who was watching. I got a lot of mileage out of that. Later I began to pretend I didn't like different foods. I remember trying to get attention about my not liking stewed tomatoes; that lasted a long time.

When I was about two or three years old I would sneak out of the house and go out in the front yard. There was a large warehouse across the street where the big freight wagons would go with their loads. Sometimes there would be four horses pulling those wagons. I used to watch as the drivers made the horses back the wagons up. The horses would be scuffling, backing up, and the drivers would be sitting on the wagon cussing at them by name. Sometimes they would lay the whip to them. That's when I learned to say, "Jack, you S.O.B.," or whatever the horse's name was that the driver thought wasn't working hard enough. I liked the cussing, but I knew better than to let anyone hear me doing it. I'd cuss to myself. I got real good at it and never got caught.

After the teamster got all parked, I would watch them go to a little old funky restaurant next door once they had tied the oat feed bag on the horses' heads. Sometimes there were fights in the place. Many times I watched as they came out drunk, stumbling around; they'd get back on their wagons, cussing, and then drive away.

Dad was a janitor then, and Mamma stayed home and took care of us four kids. She would earn extra money by making dresses for other women. She had a Singer pedal-operated sewing machine. I used to like to watch her peddling and sewing. The dresses she made were so beautiful. She made one for herself once trimmed with black sequins. While she was making the dress, which took days to finish, I was so anxious to see her in it. When she got dressed up she was the most beautiful person in the world to me. Sometimes, Dad would comb her hair, which came way down her back. He would clown around and tease her while he did it. They were so much in love.

In March of 1920, on a beautiful spring day, Dad told all four of us kids to go to another room in the house and stay there until he came for us. After what seemed like hours he finally came and told us to follow him. He led us to the bedroom where Mamma was. She was lying there in all these gleaming white bedclothes. The window was open, the gentle breeze was softly moving the curtains, Mamma was smiling, and in her arms she held a little bundle. She uncovered part of the bundle, and there was Korea. Dr. Ford stood there smiling —making sure we didn't touch her, I suppose.

Then Dad took us over to the sewing machine, where there was another bundle. Dr. Ford removed the blanket from the second baby's face. Dad told us it was Korea's twin, but she didn't make it. He told us her name; I can't remember what it was. He told us Dr. Ford would take the twin with her when she left.

About every day Mamma would make us some kind of dessert for after supper and read us a story. By this time Kenneth and Keith were both going to school, so they hung out together most of the time. Katherine and I were buddies.

Kenneth and Keith would get some of the neighbor kids together to form a parade, and they would all march down the alley behind our house, some blowing on combs with paper over them, some beating on tin cans and garbage lids for drums. All us little guys were told we were too small to be in the parade, so we stood on the sidelines as the spectators, clapping and watching. We all dreamed of being big enough to join in the parade.

Dad and Mamma took us to church at St. Stephen's. I liked to hear the choir sing. I wondered why the men made such ugly faces as they sang and the women always tried to look so cute. The preachers would tell the people about the eagle stirring his nest or one or more of the other Bible stories. I used to hear them talk about Ezekiel seeing the wheel. Then people would say, "Amen, amen." The preacher would talk so fast and loud, I wondered if they could understand what he was saying—I couldn't.

pieces 2

Leaving Denver

One Saturday morning, when I was about four and a half, we kids were shaken out of our slumber early, about sunup. Out in front of the house was a big wagon with two horses. I wondered what was happening. I soon learned we were moving. I didn't know if Kenneth and Keith knew what was going on or not, but I was really upset that no one had told me about it.

Soon Dad and some men started loading all our furniture on the wagon. When they got it all loaded, he told us kids to climb up. I had a hard time getting into the wagon. Katherine sat on the seat with Dad and Mamma. Mamma held little Korea, who was about six months old. The sidewalk was lined with all our neighbors, who had come to see us off. They were waving and saying, "Bye!" It was so much commotion you would have thought we were going a hundred or so miles away, but we were only going seven. Still, seven miles in those days was a long way.

Not many folks owned automobiles back then. A horse and buggy would take a long time going that far. I had never seen the country before—in fact, I don't think I had ever been more than a mile from where I was born—so when I saw all the cows, horses, sheep, chickens, and other farm animals, and all the open space, it was as though a miracle was happening.

We had a heavy load on the wagon, so the horses had to stop and rest two or three times along the way. Mamma had some snacks like crackers and bologna, so we all would make a sandwich and drink some soda pop while the horses rested.

Finally we got to this little house that Dad and a man named Mr. Willis had built. It was about three or four in the afternoon. Mr. Willis helped Dad unload the wagon; we kids did all we could to help. Then we were all shown the outhouse. We had never seen one before, since we had had indoor plumbing in Denver. Now we would have to go outside to pump our water from the well that Dad and Mr. Willis had dug.

So there we were, Dad, Mamma, and us five kids in a whole new environment. Dad and Mamma were determined to make this our dream home. About the only things we had were ourselves and one broken-down horse named Fred. By this time Dad had a job with the Union Pacific Railroad as a wiper. A wiper cleaned up the engines when the train came in off the track. The train engines were all steam driven then. Dad would wash them down and polish them with this black material. His hands were always black from it.

To get to work now he had to ride his bicycle the seven miles to Denver each morning and home each evening. I don't know how he did it that winter because it used to get so cold, and there was so much snow.

During that first year Dad got a couple more horses, a plow, and a few cows. I will never forget when one morning all the eggs Mamma had put in the brooder hatched. There were all these little chicks making all this racket, wanting to be fed. Mamma knew what to do. She just boiled up some eggs, chopped them up, and fed them.

By now Korea was old enough to walk and follow us around. Kenneth was about eight and a half, and Keith was going on seven. They were now going to school.

The school was a one-room schoolhouse with about twenty-five kids in it. The grades went from first to eighth. Some of the boys in the eighth grade were almost as old as the teacher. Many of the boys couldn't go to school until the crops were in. Kenneth and Keith were the only black kids in the school. Mr. Willis had two daughters the same age as Kenneth and Keith, but he had not put his girls in school.

Mr. Willis and Dad had been friends for a long time. Dad had helped him build his house, and he had helped our father build

Our one room schoolhouse seven miles from Denver, Colorado in 1920. Young Kenneth and Keith Clark to the far right. The author, Carl Clark started the following year.

ours. They played checkers almost every evening. Dad would try to persuade him to send the girls to school. Finally Dad gave up one evening and told Mr. Willis that if he wouldn't send his kids to school, he didn't want anything else to do with him. Mr. Willis didn't send them right away, and Dad kept his word. Mr. Willis eventually sent them to school, but by that time his friendship with my father was destroyed.

During this time Dad quit his job at Union Pacific because he now had the means of becoming a full-time farmer. We had about four horses and ten or twelve cows that supplied us with all the milk and butter we needed, including enough milk to sell to the dairy. We had some hogs, lots of chickens, and some guinea hens. Mamma now had improved our house. She even had a nice place to put her canning.

Dad had a cellar that we used as a smokehouse in the fall to cure the ham and bacon we had after butchering some hogs. We also kept beef there from the young cow we butchered each fall. He would put straw in the cellar so he could store potatoes, onions, squash—even a couple of watermelons.

Dad made an agreement with the Walter East store in Denver to provide them with all the tomatoes, corn, cucumbers, watermelons, cantaloupes, string beans and such that we grew.

Everything was going fine. Kenneth, Keith, and I had gotten so we could help in the fields. I was always the one Dad would put in charge of carrying in the wood and finding the chicken nests. No matter where those hens hid their nests, I would find them.

Dad bought an old broken-down racehorse to pull the buggy. The horse was beautiful but had been winded, so every mile or so she would have to stop and rest. We were slow, but we looked good. Now we had a way to go to Denver now and then so Mamma could shop and see some friends.

By that time, when I was about five or six years old, we had settled in on our little farm. We kids had become accustomed to living in the country, and due to the beautiful atmosphere our mother and father had created for us, we were extremely happy and content. Our parents had been right; they had made the right decision when we moved from Denver. All of us felt secure. Dad was singing all the time as he worked around the place. Mamma was not a good singer, but she knew how to make us feel that everything was all right.

One bright sunny morning I was playing in our front yard and heard a sound in the distance that I thought must be an airplane, though this one sounded strange. As the plane approached, I could see that it had two engines, which was why it sounded different. Planes were a novelty at that time, and I had never seen one with two engines before, so you can imagine my excitement when I saw this one flying toward me, the wind whistling through all the wire that held the wings together. Two men were sitting in the open cockpit wearing goggles and khaki uniforms. I can only guess they were in the Army. The plane was no more than fifty feet high, following the country road. As they passed I could see their faces. One of them seemed to be busy with levers and such so I came to the conclusion that he was the pilot. The other man looked at me and grinned as he waved to me. I waved back with both hands and jumped up and down with excitement, thinking, Wow, I am waving at someone who is flying! I watched as the plane disappeared down the road.

Another airplane used to pass close to our house each day going west. Someone told us it was the mail plane. One day as Keith and I watched we saw this plane make a turn toward where we were standing. We watched as it got lower and lower, then we could see it was about to land. It flew over our heads, then landed in a corn field a couple hundred feet away. We ran toward the plane as we saw the pilot get out and walk toward the farmhouse. We approached the little plane, which had two open cockpits. There were a couple of mailbags in the rear cockpit. We didn't want to disturb anything, but I felt I must touch a real airplane. Soon we observed the pilot coming back to the plane carrying a gas can. He poured the gas into the plane's tank, and Keith and I stood back and watched. He fiddled around with something in the cockpit, then he moved to the front of the plane. He grabbed the propeller, lifted one leg, and gave it a whirl. He did this several times. Suddenly the engine coughed some smoke and started. The pilot ran to the cockpit because the plane had begun to move. He let the engine run for a minute or so, then revved the motor up. He turned the plane west and it bounced noisily across the field, raising a cloud of dust and corn husks. Finally the plane lifted into the air, and Keith and I watched as it flew out of sight. I often wonder if these two experiences are the reason I became so fascinated with planes and flying.

One day I saw a group of wagons in the distance coming down our road. I had never seen anything like them before. The wagons were painted with flowers and such; even the wheels were painted in bright, beautiful colors. The horses had tassels and bells that rang as they moved at their leisurely pace. It was as though they really didn't have a destination. On one of the wagons was a man dressed in all these bright colors, playing a guitar. The women had on long, brightly colored dresses; many were smiling and some were singing. The wagon train stopped. There were about five or six wagons in front of our little house. Four or five women came to our door. Mamma seemed to be enjoying the whole thing. About two or three of the women went inside, while some stayed outside. I remember seeing one of the women outside grab a young chicken and put it in the folds of her dress. I was so mystified that the chicken didn't squawk or make any sound. I guess she knew how to stop it. They were gone after only a few minutes.

I remember Mamma telling Dad she checked the chickens after they left, and we had about five missing. The experience was worth it as far as I was concerned. I watched as they moved on down the road to the next farm so they could perform, as I saw it, their feats of magic!

By then I had started going to school. Most of the time we would walk; it was about a mile. It was all right in the spring and fall, but it was tough in the winter. I used to sit in the one-room schoolhouse and watch the teacher teaching all the older kids. I had no problem learning what she was teaching them, but for some reason I couldn't learn to read and write that first year. Mamma tried to teach me, the teacher tried, but no dice. I flunked first grade.

One day the teacher read a story. I don't remember exactly which story it was, but the word "nigger" was in it several times. Dad and Mamma had made us aware of the word. I told Mamma and the next morning she told me she was going to school with me. She put on her good coat; it was maroon in color with a fur collar. Because it had snowed she told me, "I'm going to make small steps, then you can step in my steps and you won't get wet."

Off we went to school. When we got there Mamma asked the teacher if she could talk to her. They told me to sit at my desk. I looked at them talking and smiling. My mother was a big, tall woman, and she had a smile that seemed a mile wide. After a while Mamma went home. That evening she told us kids why she had gone to the school. It was about that word "nigger." She told us the teacher had promised she would never use it again.

Dr. Ford came out to our place from time to time with her friends in a big, black, shiny car. They took Mamma on short trips and on picnics to places like Evergreen and Boulder. Mamma would bring back evergreen branches, wildflowers, and other things we had never seen. Dr. Ford usually carried a five-gallon crock on the running board of her car, and sometimes they had lemonade left over from the trip; she would always give it to us kids.

I was going through my rooster thing about that time. I would climb up on something high and let go with a loud "Cock-a-doodle-dooo!" Mamma always baked something for us, and on this day she had baked a blackberry cobbler. So as I attempted to climb up on the icebox and do my rooster, I knocked my hand against the side of the pan of cobbler that was sitting on top of the icebox; down came the cobbler, all over me and the floor. Kenneth and Keith saw the whole thing and came after me. I ran to Mamma. She picked me up and put me on her shoulder as Kenneth and Keith jumped up and down shouting, "Kill him, Mamma! Kill him!" and they meant it too. I'll have to say Mamma saved my life that day.

Even though I liked to do my rooster thing, I had a real phobia about feathers, as strange as that may sound. Anybody could run me to death with a feather. No matter how hard my mother tried to rationalize with me about how they can't hurt you and all, I still couldn't stand a feather. To this day I don't like to handle birds with feathers; they're better with no feathers and with dressing and gravy. We had one hen that would come to our screen door each day. We would let her in and she would go straight to the boys' bed and lay her egg, then make a loud cackle announcing her accomplishment before going back out. Chickens always tell everybody when they lay an egg; strange thing about those hens. I liked to hear them singing when they were content and happy. Many people don't know that chickens sing.

One day a large bull snake got under our house and began eating all the eggs in one of our chicken's nest. We ran and told Mamma. She got the old rusty pistol we owned and shot at that snake for fifteen minutes and never hit him. I wonder if she was missing him on purpose. Finally he crawled off after he had devoured all the eggs. That hen still stood there raising Cain; it didn't matter that the snake had already eaten all of her eggs. I could see the lumps of each one in his body as he crawled away.

I'll never forget the day when a swarm of bees came over our house. There were so many bees the swarm looked like a small cloud. Mamma ran inside and grabbed a dishpan and a large spoon. She came out and began to beat the pan with the spoon. It seemed like a miracle when those bees changed their course and began to circle, coming closer and closer to her. Mamma told us kids to go inside as she continued to beat on the pan. Finally the bees came down and clustered around a fence post near Mamma—there must have been thousands of them. They stayed there all night. I got up early the next morning to see if they were still there, and they were. They were waiting for the day to get warm so that they could move on. Sure enough, by mid-morning the day warmed up and they left. I watched as they kept circling until they all joined together, then off they went.

As I have been told, once they had swarmed around the post, we could have removed the queen and placed her in a beehive. The bees would have set up their home right where the queen had been placed, and we would have had our very own beehive, with plenty of honey. Mamma had the right idea, but we were unable to complete the process.

Every Saturday was bath night; we would heat water on the cookstove and pour it into a number-two tub. Katherine and Korea had to share the tub. I always thought of it as the two-kid tub, but by this time I was in the one-kid tub category. When Mamma was alive we had to bathe every Saturday, whether we needed it or not; that was the way things were in those days. On Sunday we kids looked forward to playing, and sometimes Mamma would get us ready for church and Sunday school in Denver. It was quite an experience to get five kids cleaned and dressed to go to St. Stephen's each Sunday, so Mamma could only manage the task occasionally at best.

When we were at play, our dog Jack (all our dogs were named Jack) was not allowed in the house. I wonder how those dogs endured all the petting and affection we demanding kids gave them. I would pretend to preach to the animals. It would be play, but I liked to preach to all those chickens, cows, horses, and Jack. I would stamp my feet and spread the gospel. Kenneth never got over calling me "Preach." He's done it most of his life.

Dad now let us ride to school on a horse sometimes. Kenneth would be in front, I would be in the middle, and Keith would be in back. Mamma made our lunches out of leftover fried chicken, pork chops, ham, and biscuits and such. We didn't know we had the best lunches then. We were ashamed because all the white kids had bologna, cheese, or peanut butter on light bread.

One morning the three of us were on the horse when our neighbor Roger Carr challenged Kenneth to a race to school. Away we went, neck and neck. The schoolyard gate was an arch formed by two large timbers, and there was only room for one horse to go through at a time. Traveling at full speed, both horses hit the gate at the same time. Oh what a collision! Kids, biscuits, and fried chicken filled the air. I guess God said, "I'd better take care of these fools," because no one got hurt. It was a miracle.

Winter, when I was about seven and a half, Mamma got sick and went to the hospital. She was there for about two or three weeks. Dad visited her about every other day. He would take a couple of us each time he went. He usually drove the horse and buggy into Denver, but one time when I went with him we drove over to Aurora, which was about two miles from our farm, and caught the tram. The tram was like a regular streetcar, only it had two cars hooked together. It would stop along the way picking up passengers and letting them off. As the tram arrived in Denver, we saw the Christmas trees that were all around the capitol building. When we passed the capitol we saw it was covered with many beautiful lights and decorations. I had never seen anything like it.

At the hospital, Mamma was in a long room with all the other patients. Hospitals then had large wards filled with many patients rather than separate rooms with just one or two patients each. Mamma was talking with another patient about the Bible and walking around. I wondered why she was there; she was smiling and looked the same to me. I guess we will never really know why she was there. A few days later all us kids and Dad were reciting poems and talking when a neighbor who had a phone came to our house about eight o'clock in the evening. He told Dad that Mamma had passed away. Her death certificate said "Pneumonia." I felt that I had died also. I loved her so much.

pieces 3

My Dad without Mamma

Dad gathered all us kids around him and assured us that as long as he was alive he would keep all of us together, but we had to make some adjustments. Kenneth was about twelve by now. Dad told us that when he was not around Kenneth was to take the position of leader; we were to listen to him. And Dad told Kenneth in front of us that he was to be responsible but not to bully us. Kenneth did a good job, but you can understand we didn't like it—we were kids.

By now Dad was expanding the farm, and the house was better. We had more land to grow things on, better horses, and more cows. One day Mr. Kennedy, an Irishman who was a friend of Dad's, came to our house and was talking to Dad. I happened to be close by and could hear their conversation. I remember him saying, "Hell, colored folks and Irishmen are the same. If you could turn and Irishman inside out, you would only have another colored man." Dad had a lot of respect for him and he for Dad.

As the conversation went on, he said, "You know, I got a damn horse that I'm afraid of and I got to get rid of him. Do you want him?"

"Is he any good?"

"Hell yes. That S.O.B. can out pull anything I got, only I'm afraid of him."

"What's his name?"

Mr. Kennedy kicked around in the dust, trying to avoid the question.

Dad asked again: "What's his name?"

Mr. Kennedy looked at Dad and said, "Nigger!"

Dad looked at me; I was doing all I could to keep from laughing. It tickled me that Dad had forced him to say something he didn't want to say. Dad understood that Mr. Kennedy didn't want him to take anything personally. He shook his head and said, "I'll take him."

Dad brought the horse to our place; he was as black as coal and mean as hell. He didn't want any of the other horses to get close to him, but when Dad hitched him up to a wagon with another horse, he would do his best to out pull any horse we had. We kept him two or three years. Then Dad decided he was too dangerous, so he turned him loose out on the prairie about two miles from where we lived. I saw him about a year later. He was big, black, and shiny. He had a bunch of mares and he was the king.

Mr. Kennedy came to our house again sometime later and told Dad he owned a piano that no one ever played and wanted to trade it for some geese. He made a deal with Dad that he would let him have that piano if Dad gave him five geese. Dad, thinking we needed a little culture, made the deal. After Mr. Kennedy brought the old piano over to our house, Dad would bang on it and sing almost every day. He never learned to play it, but he sure could bang on it. One day Mr. Kennedy was at our house talking to Kenneth and just kidding around with him. Kenneth kept looking down as Mr. Kennedy talked to him. After Mr. Kennedy left Dad told Kenneth, "Don't you ever let me see you looking down when someone is talking to you. Even if you are talking to the president, you look him right in the eye." I always thought that was a good lesson for me as well. I was determined to honor my father and made up my mind to look in the eye of any man who spoke to me, even if it got me in trouble. And I was also determined not to compromise any of my learned principles.

Looking back, having the piano in the house was a good idea because Dad could really sing. One day a man came to our house. Someone had told him about Dad's singing, and he said he had also heard him sing. He tried to persuade Dad to go on tour. He said he would build a show around Dad and put all us kids in it, and he declared we would all get rich.

He wanted to build a minstrel show around the family. A minstrel show was where they painted a black man's face as black as coal and make his mouth and his eyes look much larger by outlining them with white paint, so that they looked as if they were always afraid and without a brain in their heads. Al Jolsen, Eddie Cantor, Amos and Andy, and the Two Black Crows were some of the *white men* who got rich playing these characters. I'm sure Dad was aware of that when he told the man, "Hell no!" It was at this time I realized my father was stronger than I had ever imagined. I watched him make and refuse deals all the time.

I remember another time when a bootlegger who had made a deal with our neighbor to make whisky for him tried to get Dad to go into partnership with him. Dad said, "No!" The neighbor got busted and spent a year in prison. Dad stayed with farming and raising his kids.

Dad was active in the PTA at school. At first he was the only man there. He wanted to make sure us kids were treated right. We were now going to a new school they had built; each class had its own room. Dad thought it was his duty to be part of it. He was the only farmer around there who had been to college, and he was not shy about telling them. He would treat the PTA to a poem or two after the meetings. He could recite Paul Lawrence Dunbar. He also knew Wadsworth, Longfellow, and others. Sometimes he would sing them a song. Pretty soon he filled the room up when the PTA had their meetings. Men, women, and the whole countryside knew him, and most respected him.

It was around this time that someone at the school decided to put on one of those "classic" plays, as they were called. This play was about a black man who had stolen some chickens. They decided Kenneth would play the part of the chicken thief. A little blonde boy was to play the judge; another blonde boy would be Kenneth's defense. As the trial went along, Kenneth was to fall asleep. The judge at this point would rap his gavel on the bench and shout to Kenneth, "Wake up, you no-account nigger." Then Kenneth was to wake up and say, "Yes sah, yes sah." Kenneth was practicing his part at home when Dad overheard him and inquired about the play. After Dad learned what the play was all about, he gave a long lecture to Kenneth and to all of us.

Dad explained that the play was designed to make people think all black people were lazy thieves. When the black man in the play fell asleep as the lawyer tried to help him it was to show that he couldn't think for himself. The judge used the word nigger to further degrade him. "Do you understand?" Dad asked us all. "Don't ever let anyone do that to you." Those words of advice never left me. Dad told us, "You are as good as anyone else on earth, so remember that and try to be the best people you can be."

After the lecture, Dad said he was going to do something about the play. He went and bought some bologna, cheese, and crackers and such and brought it to the house. Dad told us to stay home from school the next day. He said he would be taking care of this school matter for a couple days and put Kenneth in charge. Dad was gone about three days. During that time the school was closed and the principal was fired. Dad never told us what he did, but I think about it to this day.

A few days later, shortly after dark, a group of cars drove into our front yard. They lined up so that their headlights were shining on our house. Someone shouted, "Come out here, Clark!" Dad told us kids to stay away from the windows, and he put out the lamp. When he walked out of the front door, we all peeped out the window. We were afraid for Dad; we did not want anything to happen to him. I remember seeing him move toward those lights, and finally he disappeared behind them!

We couldn't hear their conversation, but now I can imagine what went on behind those headlights. Dad probably said, "I closed that school because I want the same respect for my kids as you want for yours. I'm no troublemaker." I know someone encouraged that play because they had their own agenda—to keep black people in their place.

After what seemed like forever, Dad reappeared, walking slowly and calmly back to the house. He opened the door and walked in. The cars began to turn around and they all finally left.

Dad never said a word to us kids about what happened. I can only guess it was the KKK, because at that time they were everywhere. The NAACP was young, black folks were fighting for their rights, and the KKK was doing all they could to stop the progress. I can imagine that by being so cool Dad probably made those people ashamed of themselves, and I think that is why they didn't harm him. He had a way of making the most prejudiced and bigoted men respect him and listen to reason in his presence.

Dad was an NAACP member. He made a point of telling us about the black people who had done so much and had contributed so greatly to our country. Such as Mat Henson, who went to the North Pole with Perry, and Will Picket, a celebrated performer in Wild West shows. He dazzled audiences worldwide with his riding and roping skills, as well as his spectacular bulldogging routines. Right there in Denver was George Morrison, the musician and noted bandleader. Dad took all of us to a showing of his held at a theater in Denver. Those are just a few of the many noteworthy Negroes of that era. Dad had a good reason for making his kids aware of the black folks who had contributed so much to America. The news media and educational institutions did very little to make the public aware of such heroes, and he wanted us kids to have role models we could look up to.

My new teacher had taken enough time with me by now, and I could recite poetry, read, and spell with the best of them. One night Dad was determined to teach Kenneth fractions. Kenneth was having trouble with them, so Dad began to cut up apples to show him halves, quarters, eighths, sixteenths and such. I think Kenneth got it after about half a bushel of apples. Good thing, because Dad used them to make apple pie—so the rest of us kids were glad Kenneth had so much trouble learning fractions.

Korea was four or five, and she could recite poems right along with the rest of us and was learning everything we knew. Katherine, Korea, and I were together most of the time. Because I was their big brother, they believed anything I told them, even my lies. I would tell them about ants I had seen that were as big as houses. I told them the haystacks in our field were where they lived. And I also told them about a fish in the big ditch that was as big as a horse. Maybe they were fooling me, because I really thought they believed me.

Kenneth, Keith, and I used to swim in the big ditch. It was the water supply for all the farmers, so it was wide and deep. Connected to the big ditch was a smaller one from which we got our water. That was where Katherine and Korea were allowed to play.

One day Kenneth, Keith, and I were riding in a flatbed along the big ditch road. Kenneth was driving the two horses and stood with his legs spread apart for balance. Keith was standing the same way, and so was I. We were speeding, and Kenneth made a sharp turn. I lost my balance and fell between the wagon bed and one of the spoked wheels. The spokes hit my head like machine gun fire. My head was ringing when they got me out, but again, God saves fools. We had such a good time on that farm outside of Denver. The only time our fun was interrupted was when we had to go to Uncle Charles's house in Denver. We kids didn't like to go. Uncle Charles was the first black postman in Colorado. He was a college graduate and considered himself and his family to be aristocrats. They all looked down on us, their country cousins. There were eight kids in his family . . . none are alive today. Uncle Charles and his wife have been gone for years. And here are the country cousins as I write, in 1996, all together, and all alive and well. All of us own our own homes. Katherine is a retired school principal; Korea, a retired librarian; Keith, a retired trucker; Kenneth, a retired heavy equipment operator; and me, well, read on. . . .

pieces 4

Percy

The summer when I was about nine, Dad bought a small colt and told me he was mine. I named him Percy. He would run and play with me on those long legs and follow me around like a dog. When I whistled for him he would run to me and want to play. He grew so fast, the small, fenced-in pasture seemed smaller and smaller. I could see he wanted more and more to leave the pasture. I had been grooming and playing with him so much that by the time he got big enough to ride, I just climbed on and away we went. We could go places other than the pasture now; he seemed to really like that.

Dad had made a deal with a few of the local farmers who owned dairy cows. I would herd their cows out to a large prairie about two miles away so they could graze during the day in the summer. Each day I was to pick them up at about eight o'clock in the morning and herd them to the prairie, then bring the cows home about four o'clock in the evening so they could be milked. In all I worked about a hundred cows.

The prairie was so big it would take someone more than a day to cross it on horseback. There were wild horses, wild cattle, prairie dog towns, sagebrush, and rattlesnakes. Sometimes to amuse myself I would get a long stick and tease the rattlers. Some of them were six or seven feet long. Percy would look at me like I was a fool, and now that I think about it, I was.

The sheepherders took their sheep to the prairie in the summer. At times I saw herds of sheep, a thousand head or more, being driven down the road to the prairie. There would always be a couple of goats leading them; sheep will always follow a goat. Goats were also used to lead sheep into slaughterhouses; the dogs were there to, but mostly to keep the strays in line.

I was making about thirty dollars a month herding those cows, and I could say I was a real cowboy. Most of the money went to Dad. He did let me buy a fancy bridle for Percy, some cuffs, and a cowboy hat, but I never got a saddle. I really didn't need one; I used only a blanket. By now I could stand up on Percy and let him run as fast as he could; I seldom fell off.

I usually had to climb onto Percy's back from a fence or something because I was so small and Percy was by now a full-grown horse. Sometimes he would put his head down and let me shinny up his neck. When I got up on his neck, he would lift his head up and I would slide down his neck onto his back. Sometimes, just to be ornery, he wouldn't put his head down for me, so I would just grab his reins and lead him to a place where I could mount him, but when he did lower his head he would turn his ears back toward me, awaiting my orders.

It finally got so he could predict what I wanted and even got so he knew which cows belonged to which farm, so all I had to do was leave it up to him. If one of those cows didn't do what they were supposed to, he would give them a little bite on their butt and that would straighten them out. I loved that horse and he loved me.

There was one herd of wild cows that had a big white bull as their leader. Every time he saw Percy and me he would start pawing the earth, throwing dust over his back, as if to say, "Stay away from me and my cows." He would do this even if we were a quarter mile or more away. Sometimes he charged after us. We always turned and ran away, then he would turn around and go back to his cows. . . . I hated him!

One day, when I went to bring the cattle home, he was close to my cows. As soon as he saw us he started pawing and snorting. I should have known to stay away, but I rode Percy right up to him. I said to him, "I'm not afraid of you!" All of a sudden he charged old Percy and lifted us both off the ground. When Percy came down I fell off. There I stood, facing the bull, this little ten-year-old boy. Percy could have run off, but he stood there between the bull and

Impression of my pony, Percy.

me. I was so frightened. I couldn't believe I was on the ground; I could only think, "If Percy leaves me, this bull is going to kill me!" The bull pawed in the dust and looked at me under Percy's belly. I pleaded, "Percy, please don't leave me. Percy!" I had never been so scared in my life.

Suddenly, out of nowhere, a cowboy appeared, a real one with spurs, bullwhip, and all. He had a dog with him. They attacked the bull. The dog bit the bull on his legs and the cowboy laid that long bullwhip across his back. I couldn't believe my eyes; everything seemed unreal, happening in some kind of slow motion. That bull-whip was snapping and the dog was biting and growling and there stood Percy in all the dust and confusion, his attention split between the bull and me. Suddenly it ended. The bull took flight.

I saw the perfect moment to get on Percy's back and run. Percy wanted to do the same. He lowered his head; I could feel the strength in Percy's neck as he brought me to his back. He stepped to and fro as if to follow my head movements as I looked for the bull and for that cowboy and his dog. From Percy's back I could see the bull running to his cows, but nowhere could I see the cowboy. I was still filled with fear from the bull, and dust was still in the air, but the cowboy was gone.

I shouted, "Percy, take me home!" He ran so fast, it wasn't long before we were home. . . . I know to this day that there must have been some kind of divine intervention, because the prairie was so flat I should have seen anybody within five miles, but the cowboy had completely disappeared, without saying a word to me. I was afraid to tell Dad about the incident because I knew he would stop me from herding cows, and I knew if I said anything to anybody about that cowboy they would think I was crazy.

A few weeks later, as I was looking for my cows, I saw the bull again with his cows about a quarter mile or more away. I did not want any part of him, and just as we turned to run away, Percy stumbled and I fell off. I kept trying to get Percy to drop his head and let me climb back on, but Percy for some reason would not let me. I tried to lead Percy to a place where I could mount him, but he was paying too much attention to that bull. I started to pull harder and harder on his reins . . . he just would not run with me.

Suddenly I saw the bull coming closer. This time he didn't stop and paw in the dust as he had in the past—he came running at full speed, dust flying, directly toward us. The bull was running so fast that Percy's attention was all on him and not me. Percy still wouldn't lower his head to let me on or run with me. I tried to get Percy to let me up on him one more time, but he wouldn't. In the confusion, I turned Percy loose and just started running.

I knew of a pipe a short distance away that ran under an old abandoned railway. I prayed I could get there before the bull caught me. I finally reached the pipe and slipped in backwards. I had to be very careful not to go too far back in the pipe because it dropped down about twenty feet on its way under the railway track. God I was scared. I knew if I fell in I would never get out. So there I was, about two feet from the end of the pipe, praying the bull would not find me.

All of a sudden there was this big head—it was over a foot

wide—with big, bulging eyes that were looking in at me . . . we were face to face. The bull started to paw at the pipe. I was frozen; I felt as though I was part of the pipe. I knew I couldn't back up any further. Where are you, Percy? I thought.

As the bull pawed at the end of the pipe, he bent it smaller and smaller. I was as worried about him making the pipe so small I wouldn't be able to get out as I was worried about him getting in. Every now and then the bull would stop pawing at the old tin pipe, lower his head, and gaze at me only a foot or so away. His hot breath and the mucous from his nose were all over my face. He just stared at me; he seemed to be trying to figure out how to get to me.

Finally, after what seemed an eternity, he stopped. I prayed he had given up and gone away. I waited and waited, afraid to try to get out of the pipe because he might still be there.

After a while I squeezed my head through the opening; I couldn't see him. I figured I had better wait there a couple of minutes to see what the bull was up to. I could hear some movement outside the pipe. Please, bull, just go away, I thought to myself.

A face came to the pipe. It was Percy. He put his head down and smelled my face, as if to see if I was all right. I squeezed out. The bull was running back to his cows; they were going away. Percy put his head down, I climbed on, and we went to catch up with my cows, which had started toward home.

Several evenings passed before I went after those cows again, and when I did, I looked and looked but could not find them. The sun was going down, and I didn't know which direction was home. Every time Percy tried to lead me in one direction I made him go another way—I don't know why.

The sun was down now and the moon was bright. Rattlesnakes were everywhere. The owls were out. I didn't have any idea where I was. I really didn't panic at first until I looked around and realized we were in an old graveyard. The moonlight was shining on the old crosses and headstones, and on all those sunken graves. The one next to Percy and me had a whole nest of rattlesnakes in it. They were crawling all over one another.

That's when I finally gave Percy his head and told him, "Take us home, Percy!" Percy immediately turned in the right direction and we rode like the wind. I had left home at about three-thirty the day before to get the cows, and Percy led me back to the entrance to the prairie at around four o'clock in the morning.

About a mile away were the headlights of a dozen or so cars. I wondered if it was my dad and some of our neighbors looking for me. As I rode closer to the lights I heard someone shout, "I think I see him." Dad came running toward me, calling my name. When I answered, he yelled to the others, "It's him, my son, thank God." Dad lifted me from Percy's back, hugging me while repeating, "Thank God you are all right."

The others milled about, reassuring Dad and asking me questions. I could make out some of their faces—Mr. Kennedy, Mr. Kemp, Roger Carr, and others who I recognized but whose names I didn't know. I felt good that these men had enough respect and compassion for me and my father to get up so early in the morning and come to his aid. I wondered if some of them had been at our house a year ago when those men came to talk to Dad after he closed the school.

Dad thanked the men. They began to get into their cars and start toward their homes. Percy stood there watching all that was going on. Dad asked me if I could bring Percy home; I told him I felt fine and I could. Dawn was just beginning to break as Dad got into a Model T with one of the men and started for home. Percy and I watched as the taillights slowly disappeared down the road. Percy went into a gentle gallop as we followed. I began to think about the whole thing. Would Dad still let me herd the cows after this? Would he lose his confidence in me? I hoped he would let me continue my job. I was sure this wouldn't happen again.

Finally we arrived home. I dismounted Percy, removed his blanket and bridle, gave him a pat or two on the neck. As I walked toward our house, I looked back at Percy. He was just standing there watching as I walked away. I can imagine he was trying to sort it all out the same as I, hoping everything would be okay. Somehow I talked Dad into letting me continue herding the cows until later that fall.

Keith and the girls wanted to see me and Percy ride after hearing all the stories. I went way down to the back of our yard, stood up on Percy, and told him, "Go!" Percy ran across the yard as fast as he could while I stood on his back. Keith knew there was a clothesline across the yard that day, but I didn't. When I hit that clothesline, I must have flew twenty feet in the air. When I landed they were all laughing; it seemed as though everyone had known about the clothesline but me. Luckily again, I didn't get hurt or killed. God is good.

One day when I went out to get Percy, I grabbed him by the tail as I always had since he was a colt. He raised both hooves and kicked me in the face. After he kicked me, he turned around and looked at what he had done. I was bleeding from a gash under my eye. He smelled my face and just stood there. Dad said that was enough. Soon after, Percy was gone. Dad never told me what happened to him. I have a scar under my right eye to this day. Every time I see it, I think about Percy.

"Impression," painted by the author imagining how the family looked at various times, living in separate places after they were orphaned.

pieces 5

Family Split

By now we were all going to school. Dad was true to his word about keeping us together. We were happy he had bought a Model T Ford and had converted it into a truck. Keith was the designated driver to haul the produce to town and take the milk to the dairy. He was only twelve years old but big for his age. In those days no one had to have a driver's license. Dad never learned to drive. We were raising sugar beets now as our primary crop. Life was good, but Dad worked much too hard. Still, he always found time to do things with us. We went to all the plays at the school. In the summer he took us to Denver. He even took all of us to an opera once. I used to really like it when he took us to see animal acts on stage and in the circus.

In December of 1927 Dad got extremely ill with pneumonia. He held on as long as he could. Then, in the bitter cold of one December morning, he told Kenneth and Keith to start the car so they could take him to the hospital in Denver. As they tried to start the Model T Ford in the bitter cold, Dad sat with Korea, Katherine, and me in back of the stove on a bench; that was the only heat we had. He was trying to put on his socks when he gently rolled over onto my lap and died. I was eleven, old enough to know what was happening. After the loss of our last parent, no one would be able to take care of all of us, as many people were barely making it themselves.

Dad's funeral was at St. Stephen's church. The choir sang. It was raining heavily. There was no family car; I was in the car with the Smiths, friends of my father. It was raining so hard, and it was so cold, they told me to stay in the car when we got to the grave site. The rain was running down the windows of the car. The weather was so dark and bleak. It took me a long time to get over the deep sorrow. I would remember how when we were out in the field Dad would tell me, "Carl, go up to the house and see if those beans are jumping over one another." If they weren't, I was to put a couple more lumps of coal on the fire. If the beans turned out good, he would say, "Them beans are so good, they will make you slap yo mamma!" I would go away by myself and cry, thinking of him.

Aunt Lizzie was there at the funeral all the way from St. Joseph, Missouri. She stayed in Denver with her brother, our Uncle Charles, for a few days. When she left to go back home, she and Uncle Charles decided she would take Korea, who was seven, to live with her. The next time I saw Korea she was in her twenties. Keith and I went to live in Denver with Dad's other brother, Uncle Henry. He had eight kids of his own. Katherine lived with Uncle Charles for a year, then Mrs. Toomer, a friend of Aunt Lizzie's in St. Joseph, Missouri, agreed to take Katherine, who was then about nine. The next time I saw Katherine she was also in her twenties. Kenneth was just about on his own; he was fifteen.

The next spring Uncle Charles sent us three boys—three kids—back out to run the farm. I was still only eleven. Kenneth and Keith put me back in school full time. They would go when they could, because we still had cows, horses, and all the rest to care for. A good neighbor up the road had been taking care of the animals and keeping an eye on the place while we were in Denver.

Not long after we came back to the farm, I got sick. One morning Kenneth and Keith were out taking care of some farm chores; I was feeling so bad I must have been delirious. I gazed out the window at a patch of green moss on the ground. It looked so tempting, I went out and lay down on it, not realizing the ground under it was still frozen. I don't know how long I lay there, but the next thing I remember, these two black folks, Mr. and Mrs. Loggins, whom I had never seen before, picked me up off the ground and told me I was coming with them. They wrapped me up in a blanket and put me in their Model T Ford. By the time we got to their house, which was about fifteen miles away, I was unconscious. I was that way for three days, until they brought me back to health. I didn't know it at the time, but they had made a deal with Uncle Charles in Denver—he was to give them some money for my room and board. For some reason Uncle Charles didn't live up to his end of the bargain.

Mr. and Mrs. Loggins were illiterate sharecroppers, although they did put me in school. It was a small schoolhouse with a lot of white kids. I was the first black that some of the kids at this school had ever seen. I had to fight a lot at first, because they knew all the names—coon, darky, nigger, black cloud, and all the rest. I'd go crazy when I got in a fight with those kids. Soon they thought it was better to get along with me than to call me any of those names. I stayed there with the Logginses until I was about sixteen. They had me read the paper to them and just plain worked the hell out of me on the farm. The next spring I worked with them in the fields. They grew sugar beets mostly. Mr. and Mrs. Loggins would cut eight-inch-long blocks of young beets along the row, leaving behind a little patch of plants. It was my job to crawl along behind them and thin the little patches, leaving one plant. I had kneepads made out of gunnysacks. I bet I have crawled the distance from California to New York up and down those rows. I had corns on my knees and the knuckles of my hands for fifteen years afterward. Of course I also had to do all kinds of other daily chores, like chopping wood, bringing in coal, and collecting eggs. The only chore I didn't have was milking the cow; Bossie refused to let me milk her.

While all this work was going on, Mr. Loggins beat me about once a month. I don't mean spank or whip, I mean beat like a dog. I have scars to this day from those beatings. I think they beat me because of their frustration over Uncle Charles not paying them as he had promised. I'd hear about it constantly.

The fact that I was the only black kid in an all-white school didn't help me much either. Each morning after the Pledge of Allegiance there would be a session of about three songs. Most of the songs were by Stephen Foster: "Massa in the Cold, Cold Ground," "My Old Kentucky Home," and "Old Black Joe." All the songs told about how black folks were so happy to serve and at the same time be abused by "Ole Massa." I knew better, and because I knew better it would really mess up my day. One time, while the class was singing "Ole Black Joe," I got caught saying "Ole Black-Ass Joe." I didn't mean for the teacher, Miss Mack, to hear me, but she did. I guess I was really enjoying myself; I had always sung it my way but this time I got caught. When Miss Mack asked me why I sang that way, I told her why. I said it was because I hated those songs. She said to me calmly and with what felt like compassion, "I understand."

About that time Uncle Charles decided to take Kenneth and Keith off the farm. He sent Keith to Kansas City to live with our mother's sister, Aunt Mary. So now only Kenneth and I were in Colorado. Kenneth worked wherever he could to make a living. He even lived with me at the Logginses for awhile.

I was about fifteen now, in high school at East Lake. Mrs. Loggins bought me a ten-dollar violin. I already knew how to read music, so after I got one free lesson, I was on my way. Miss Mack insisted I join the school band.

The Logginses took me to town with them almost every week. I usually visited Kenneth, who was about twenty and had gotten married to a woman named Mary. He always asked me, "Preach, how things going?" I always said, "Fine." Other times I visited Uncle Charles or Uncle Henry. I always asked my cousins if I could ride their bicycles; I never owned one myself. At times I went to a ten-cent movie, and sometimes the Logginses, after buying groceries on Saturday, went to Welton Street, the main drag in the colored part of town, and we would just sit there in that old car eating salmon sandwiches (*simon*, as she pronounced it) with cheese and drinking orange pop and just watching the city folks.

There was not enough time for me to do anything else, so I would be there as well watching the city folks and listening to the Logginses talk about everybody that walked by. Mrs. Loggins would comment, "These young gals and those short skirts," then she would state to Mr. Loggins, "Ain't it a shame, those gals in them short skirts!"

I saw how he enjoyed watching, but he always said, "Yeah, sho is a shame." I, being about fifteen years old, had my own thoughts about "those gals," as Mrs. Loggins called them. Those short skirts were all right with me. I could only laugh to myself about Deacon Loggins, who was getting so much pleasure out of them.

Every few weeks there was a Saturday parade down Welton Street. There were people in those parades who represented just about all aspects of the community—barbecue restaurants, barbershops, shoe-shine parlors, and the like.

The White Elephants, who were members of the Negro League, were there with their baseball uniforms on. I often heard about how the owner of the White Elephants said he always had to get several of his players out of jail so they could play on Sunday. Sundays they played all the great Negro teams, like the Kansas City Monarchs and the Homestead Grays, with Satchel Paige, the Big Train, Josh Gibson, and other star athletes of the day.

New Hope Baptist Church, Porter Funeral Home, St. Stephen's, all were represented in the parade. There would be two or three bands playing ragtime. I will always remember the bands with their trombones, trumpets, peck horns, and drums, and how they could march and strut; it was a sight to behold. The sisters from the churches would be marching and sweating, wobbling on their high heels. Many weren't very good at walking in them; after all, they only wore them to church on Sunday. Granberry and Campbell Mortuary would always be there; they had all the best cars for the preachers and such to ride in. I suppose they felt all those people would be their customers sooner or later.

Now and then, the press printed something in the newspapers about the parade. They would comment about all the raggedy cars and such, unless it was close to an election, when they courted the colored folks for votes; then they would write something nice.

Sometimes there was a rally on the corner, at Five Points, where people would address certain issues. One rally in particular I remember was for raising funds for the Scottsboro Boys, to keep them from being "legally" lynched in the South. I think there were five of them.

On Sunday I'd go to church with the Logginses. They usually went someplace afterward. Sometimes they went to the home of another church member. Sometimes they went to some other friend's house, where the music played and the home brew flowed. Whenever the home brew flowed, the little old flivver Mr. Loggins drove would be all over the road, all the way home. I knew then that he had drunk too much. I'd be sitting there frozen, afraid to say a word.

Mr. Loggins raised a turkey named Gobbler. He was a big rascal and he knew I was afraid of him. I was not really afraid of what he could do to me, but it was that old feather thing again. Every time he saw me walk through the door he would put his wings down and come after me. Finally I had to carry around a stick; he was afraid of that. One day the Logginses went to town. Whenever they left me home alone I made a big batch of cookies. I'd put them in a coffee can and hide them in the barn. I had made a batch and was on my way to the barn when that old Gobbler came after me.

I didn't have my stick, so I picked up a rock and threw it at him. I hit him right in the head and he toppled over dead. Now I knew that if Mr. Loggins found out I had killed Gobbler, I would be dead too, so I took him way out in the field and buried him. Mr. Loggins asked me a few days later if I'd seen Gobbler. I told him, "I haven't, but a few nights before I saw a coyote in our yard; maybe he got him." He must have believed me because he never asked again.

There was a cornfield right by my window, and the nearest corn stalks were only two or three feet away. Believe me, at night, in hot weather, I could hear that corn grow. I slept on a straw pallet; in the daytime I rolled it up and put it in a closet.

The beatings came more frequently once I turned sixteen. Even Mrs. Loggins got in on it. One night she decided to get her licks in while I was sleeping on my pallet. She gathered a handful of switches and put them in the fire to get them good and hot. I was sleeping in a nightshirt; she pulled my nightshirt up and starting beating me. Some of those switches had fire on them. They caught my pallet on fire. We had to throw it out in the snow to put the fire out.

Around eight-thirty each night, after I got through with all my chores, such as washing the dishes after we ate supper, I had to complete homework in all my subjects. Sometimes I nodded off. Mrs. Loggins would put broom straws in my eyelids to keep them open. It didn't do any good; I just slept with my eyes open. Mr. Loggins didn't talk to me except when he had some kind of criticism, or to raise hell with me.

The Logginses decided to take me out of school and put me to work full time. I had nowhere to go. Kenneth and his wife were having a hard time making ends meet themselves.

One day Mr. Loggins beat me with a big harness strap he had made into a whip. He beat me for so long I thought he was going to kill me. He told me, "You are either going to cry or I'm going to kill you!"

There on my knees in front of him I said to myself, Go on, kill me! I won't cry. Finally he stopped. I put my hand behind my back; my hand filled with blood. I thought, This is it, I'm running away tomorrow morning.

Later that day Mrs. Loggins told me, "We don't want you here. If we had known your uncle wasn't going to give us any money, we wouldn't have brought you here to begin with. Why don't you run away?" Although I was sixteen, I was about the size of a twelve-year-old. That was one of the reasons I took the abuse for so long; I was so small for my age.

That night I put the clothes I was going to take with me in a shirt. I tied them up and pushed them under the bed—I had a bed by then. I had about two dollars that I had saved up. Then I lay across the bed waiting for the freight train that came by our house at four-thirty every morning. It would always slow as it went up the grade by our house. I didn't know where I was going, and I didn't care.

About three o'clock in the morning there came a knock on our door. Mr. Loggins got his shotgun and answered the door. I heard Kenneth's voice. He said, "Mr. Loggins, I have come for Carl. My wife Mary said my mother came to her in a vision and told her to go get Carl; he is going to run away this morning."

Mr. Loggins came to my room. I'd never seen him look like that; he looked so small and pathetic. He asked me, "You plan to run away, boy?"

I told him, "Yes."

He said, "How far you going, as small as you is?"

I replied, "Because you and Mrs. Loggins have mistreated me ever since I've been here, I don't want to see you ever again." As I looked at him, he did something I was almost sure he was incapable of: a tear ran down his face. I thought, Suffer, that's only your guilt. As I went to get my few belongings, Mrs. Loggins, who had been quietly watching everything, came into the room and tried to hand me my violin. I looked at her and felt sorry for her because I think she loved me but didn't know how to treat me. I said, "No, I don't want it." She just stood there looking as small and sad as Mr. Loggins.

pieces 6

Back to Denver

Kenneth and I got into his little old car and off to Denver we went. I thought to myself, I know this can't be any worse. I didn't look back. I never went to see the Logginses there again, though I did go see Mrs. Loggins in Oakland, California, a little more than ten years later. At that time I was twenty-seven or twenty-eight years old. She told me I owed her for taking care of me way back then. She hadn't thought about all that work I did, or the way they had beat the hell out of me. She was the same illiterate sharecropper, only living in Oakland now.

Kenneth and Mary lived on Glenarm in Denver in a two-bedroom apartment. We had two beds, one chair in the kitchen, and a cookstove that burned coal. Our light was a kerosene lamp. In the winter, when dinner was over, we had to sit in the kitchen to keep warm. We had only one chair, so when we all sat down at the same time Mary had to sit in Kenneth's lap, and I would sit on an orange crate we had found someplace. We amused ourselves by singing, telling stories, or reading poetry. We were too poor to have a radio. One day we decided to turn the electricity on ourselves, so we connected the wires in the fuse box. Amazingly, we had lights! The power company never checked on us.

This was the middle of the Great Depression. People were starving and freezing to death on the streets. Kenneth and I did odd jobs and made enough money to get by. I had a couple of apartment houses where I would stoke the furnace and sweep up. Then I would walk downtown to the *Denver Post*, buy about twenty newspapers, and sell them on the street.

Kenneth and Mary put me back in school at Manuel High. I had almost no clothes, so I wore the same old raggedy coat day after day. I began to get on my feet later that summer. The number of people who I did odd jobs for increased, so finally I asked Kenneth if I could buy a new suit. I had saved up twenty-five dollars. He told me it was okay, but only if I could pay cash for it. I went to Sears and bought a dark green suit, the first new suit I had ever owned. I was so proud of myself.

The same week that I bought the suit Kenneth and Mary planned to go to Boulder, about thirty miles away, for a church picnic. Mary had to ride with the Richardsons, some friends of theirs from church. I told Kenneth I would ride with him in his Model T Ford. He had cut it down and made it into a runabout.

At the picnic all the young guys and girls were looking at me in my new suit. I was so proud of myself and doing a little strutting, I'm sure. Right before dark we headed back to Denver. About the time we got to the outskirts of Denver, the Model T stopped . . . out of gas. Kenneth and I got out to push it further off the highway. Kenneth pushed from the back, I leaned in through the side, pushing and steering, and we finally got the car rolling. Kenneth had started to leave to go get some gas and I was still pushing when *wham!*—a car hit us from behind going full speed. It knocked me out onto the highway, unconscious. Kenneth ran back, picked me up, and carried me off the road. When I came to, the first thing I remember saying is, "Look at my new suit!" The arm was ripped off, and the pant leg was ripped too. I didn't notice that there was a hole all the way through my face and blood was all over me. The man in the other car was bruised up, but he was okay. He and Kenneth stopped the bleeding from my face. Then from somewhere the police came. They took us all downtown to the jailhouse.

When we got there the police took the man who had hit us into another room. After they talked to him, they told us the man had asked them to let us go. He said he knew we didn't have any money, so there was no point in putting Kenneth in jail, even though something about the car lights and the license was not right.

We had to walk home, all the way from downtown. People stared at us. Here I was with blood all over me and my new clothes torn up.

When we walked into the house, Mary was already there. She almost fainted when she saw me. All I could think of was how my new suit was ruined.

Kenneth got on the WPA, a program started by President Roosevelt to put people to work. Up until this time there were few jobs. White folks as well as black were working any job they could just for food and board. A black man was very lucky if he could get a job as a Pullman porter on the railroad, or a porter in a hotel, or a handyman at someone's house. Women were mostly maids and cooks. By law, freight trains transported jobless people across the country to try and find work. Kenneth bought himself a nice Chevrolet, though. You could buy a new one for about five hundred dollars. Kenneth had about a hundred-dollar car.

We moved to a house where we didn't have to go outside to the toilet, and Kenneth bought a radio for Mary. I was still doing odd jobs, and we were doing pretty well. We even had some half-decent furniture. I was going to high school and had been able to make some friends. I went to church each Sunday. Life was okay.

pieces 7

Civil Conservation Corps

In 1936, when I was nineteen, Kenneth learned about the Civil Conservation Corps (CCC) and got me a job there. The camp was about twenty miles away up in the mountains, and I went home almost every week. We built stone walls and a real log-cabin lodge, removed trees, and made roads. We actually built a park. Bears, elk, deer, mountain lions, bobcats—all would wander through our camp. I loved it.

They paid me thirty dollars a month. I got five dollars in scrip, which I could only use at camp; the other twenty-five dollars I sent home to Kenneth. When payday came, all the men who didn't have families outside the camp were paid in cash, so there was a lot of gambling. I had seen some gambling on Welton Street in Denver but had never done it. That was about to change.

There was a black preacher in camp who loved to gamble, but he didn't want to touch the dice. He made a deal with me: if I rolled the dice for him, he would make the bets. I agreed. The first game we were in he won about fifty dollars betting on me. Every time I won he would look up toward heaven and say, "Thank you, Lord," then he would put down his next bet. At the end he gave me five one-dollar bills. I thought, This is all right. He started me gambling, and I loved it very much. I gambled all through my Navy career—I made big money too.

Every Friday evening after dinner they showed a movie. Many were about the Navy. The sailors in those movies would go to all these exotic places and have fun; the films never showed them working. I began to think I would like to do that. I wanted to travel and do all the things I saw them do.

So, after watching all those Navy movies at the camp, one of my buddies and I finally decided we wanted to join. Though I was nineteen at the time, I still had to get permission from Kenneth. I told him what I wanted to do. Kenneth said he would think about it and let me know by the next week, when I came home from the CCC. He reluctantly agreed to let me join. I told my buddy at the camp, Cruse, who was Mexican, and he decided he would sign up with me. The next Friday Cruse and I went to the Navy Recruiting Office, which was located inside the Denver Post Office. As we walked down the marble hallways we looked for the Navy sign. Finally we found the place. We entered and saw a man sitting at a desk directly in front of us. We had never before seen a Navy person with a uniform like this man had; with all the gold on his sleeve and such, he looked to us like somebody really important. Now I can imagine he was probably a chief petty officer. He was all smiles as he asked if he could do something for us. I said, "We are here to join the Navy."

The officer looked at Cruse and said, "I'm sorry, but you can't join."

Cruse asked, "Why not? I'm an American citizen."

The officer repeated, "I'm sorry."

Cruse stood there for a moment, waiting for an explanation. The officer looked at him without saying another word. I could see the pain in Cruse's face as he slowly turned and walked away. I thought maybe I should leave too because I felt so bad.

I stayed, though, and the officer walked me into another room, where there were some small tables and chairs. Two other black men were sitting there. The officer introduced me to them. He then gave each of us some sheets of paper with questions on them that we were to answer. I can remember that one of the questions was, What do you plan to be in the Navy? There were several choices. One was electrician, which was what I chose.

The officer then sent us to another room, where we were given a physical examination. The doctor poked us, looked at our teeth, and afterwards pronounced that we were fit for the US Navy. We waited in a third room until the officer came to tell us we had been accepted and should return the following Friday to be sworn in. I went back to my job in the CCC, but all I could think about was next Friday, when I would be in the Navy.

By now Kenneth was not so sure about the whole thing and tried to talk me out of it. I stuck to my guns, and he finally said okay. The next Friday I arrived on time. The recruiting officer told us he was going to swear us in and have us sign some papers. He lined the three of us up, and we repeated the oath after him. Then he said, "I want to congratulate you all; you are now mess attendants in the United States Navy."

We said, "What's a mess attendant?"

He told us, "You have one of the best jobs in the Navy. You will be taking care of the officers—making up their beds, feeding them their meals, shining their shoes—and the good part is, you don't have to eat what the other sailors eat; you will be eating the same food as the officers."

I said, "I don't want to be no mess attendant! I put in those papers I want to be an electrician!"

He bellowed, "Attention!" We didn't know how to stand at attention, so he showed us. Then he told us, "You are now in the Navy and subject to all the rules, regulations, and orders." He told us that the consequences for not following those rules, regulations, and orders were brig or prison time with hard labor. I thought, What the hell have I gotten myself into? I can't get out of this now for four years.

The officer told us to be back at the recruiting office at nine o'clock Monday morning, and if we weren't, he would court martial us. I was sure to get there on time Monday. I didn't tell Kenneth and Mary what had happened, only that I had to be there Monday morning, and I was leaving for San Diego, California. Kenneth surprised me when he took me down to the recruiting office to see me off. He handed me an envelope; in the envelope was all the money I had sent home from the CCC—two hundred and fifty-five dollars. He said, "This is yours. Good-bye, Preach!" The recruiter gave us thirty dollars and our tickets for the Santa Fe Railway. A Navy car drove us to the station, and we were off to San Diego.

pieces 8

US Navy / Boot Camp

I had never been on a train before. I was very excited to see all the new scenery. I stayed awake all night as we went through the mountains and prairies. When morning came we were in New Mexico. The Santa Fe had restaurants along the line called Harvey Houses where the train would pull in and wait until the passengers could get off to eat and buy Indian souvenirs. The Indians would be in their native dress—lots of beads and bright colors.

By now I was a full-blown gambler thanks to that preacher. I had won most of my buddies' money the night before, so I bought them breakfast; it was the best I had ever had. As we passed through California with its green trees, green grass, and flowers blooming, I saw ladies hanging out their wash on the line—no dryers back then. With all the lemon and orange trees in people's back yards, it seemed like a wonderland. I had just left all that snow and cold in Denver.

We reached San Diego at about two or three o'clock in the afternoon. I could see all the ships in the harbor; they seemed so big. Most were anchored. I itched to be aboard one of them, traveling all over the world. I only hoped I could put up with the demeaning mess attendant business I had gotten myself into. I knew I would have to try to make the best of it.

An officer unloaded us from the train. There were some young white fellows going into the Navy on the train also. There were about fifteen of us blacks in all. The officer told us to line up by the train with our bags. A sailor took charge. He marched us to a Navy bus. He loaded all the white boys first, then he loaded the few of us black boys. He told us to proceed to the back of the bus. Then we were off to training camp, which was called boot camp by the sailors.

When we arrived at camp, the white boys were unloaded first; another sailor took them under his control. The bus took us to another part of the camp, where we were to stay separated from the white boys. We were marched to a barracks, where they issued us all our clothes, a hammock, and bedding—at that time, in 1936, many Navy ships still had the sailors sleep in hammocks. Then, after we got all our instructions, we were marched to our quarters. We tried on our Navy uniforms; mine was two sizes too big. They told us we would fill them up by the time we left boot camp, and we did.

Each day we were drilled for eight hours. There were only fifteen of us black boys, and we were totally segregated from the white boys. Because there were so few of us, the instructor could give us special attention. After a few weeks we were the best at drilling in boot camp. Every day as we drilled, we had an audience of several officers and their families. They didn't look at the white boys. I sometimes wondered if they wanted to see if we had enough intelligence to learn those intricate maneuvers. I believed we were an experiment—most of those people had not been around black people before.

When we were marched down to the mess hall, we stood at attention until we were told to sit. We were given fifteen minutes to eat. Me being a slow eater, I could never finish before they gave us the command to rise and marched us out. I would look longingly at all the food I had to leave at almost every meal.

As the fifteen of us went through our boot camp training, there were eleven other black guys who had completed boot camp and were working in the galley and mess hall. They were assigned there until we were through training so the Navy could put all twenty-six of us on a ship and send us to Norfolk, Virginia, where we would learn how to shine shoes, polish silver, set tables, and do all the things the Navy decided we should know to be good mess attendants.

When our three months were over in San Diego, they put us all together and prepared us to board the USS *Chaumont*, an old, rusty ship the Navy used to haul personnel and goods. At that time the Navy only had about three transport ships. The government was

This is the first day in Boot Camp. I'm on the left bottom.

about as poor as the rest of the country; the Depression was affecting everything everywhere. As we approached the ship, I was able to see just how big it really was. Because of its size, I felt that if I was prone to seasickness, I would be okay. This illusion was soon proven wrong. The very first day at sea I got so sick, I couldn't imagine it being any worse. I think my stomach turned inside out. I lay up there on the deck so sick I couldn't even move for two days. When the deck crew washed the deck down, they just washed me like I was a part of the ship, or an old, dirty rag. If I could have moved to the side of the ship, I think I would have jumped over.

Finally, on the morning of the third day, a white sailor, one of the old salts, came to my aid. He had a pitcher of lemonade and half a loaf of hot baked bread that he had buttered. He poured me a glass of lemonade, held my head up, and helped me drink it. Then he broke off a big chunk of that hot bread and fed it to me. After a couple of glasses of lemonade and some more bread, I began to feel a lot better; I ate and drank it all. I got up and thanked him, suddenly realizing how filthy I was from vomiting all over myself. I went down and asked someone where, and how, I could clean up.

In those days the ship issued each sailor one bucket of fresh water per day. Out of that you had to wash yourself, then rinse with seawater. Your clothes had to be washed with the fresh water that was left over. We slept in hammocks, which had to be taken down each morning. The master-at-arms (ship's police) would wake us by going to each compartment on the ship, accompanied by his big bulldog, who hated black folks. As the master-at-arms whacked us on the butt with his stick, that damn dog would bark, growl, and show us his teeth.

I often still think about that dog; he was the ugliest damn dog I have ever seen. Some sailors had brought him up on the ship and now he seemed to think he was a sailor. When they took him off the ship he had his own sailor suit, his own liberty card, and his own ID. When the sailors went into bars to get drunk, he drank beer right along with them. He would stagger back aboard ship just as drunk as they were. In those days, getting drunk and fighting was condoned and encouraged. It was the mark of being a good sailor. As I recall, the dog didn't have a name—he was just "Dog."

It took us about ten or eleven days to get to the west coast of Panama, the first stop on our trip from San Diego to Norfolk, Virginia. We were allowed to go ashore. The officers were given shore leave and the enlisted men were given liberty. The two guys from Denver and I went to town. I had never seen anything like it. In those days the town had designated an area about three blocks long where all the prostitutes and hustlers could operate freely. The prostitutes would sit in the window and call to us sailors. "Three ways for a dollar" were their terms. The three of us, who had been lying to each other about how worldly we had been in Denver, now had to put up. I found they were as scared as I was. Finally we went into one of those places. I did not have any money with me to speak of except for some change. I lost my virginity for thirty-five cents in Balboa, Panama.

One afternoon in Panama, Dog was in a bar with his shipmates drinking beer. All of a sudden a female dog that must have been in heat passed by. Dog must have gotten a whiff, because he took off after her, and I can imagine him saying, "See you on the ship, fellas.

Nature calls!" as he and the female disappeared.

Well, liberty was coming to an end; most of us were back on board ship. We heard that Dog had not made it back. The captain dispatched a search party for Dog and delayed our departure; we obviously weren't leaving until Dog was aboard ship. Apparently there were some other male dogs in the vicinity, because when Dog was found, he was a mess. He had obviously been in at least one fight, and it must have been a good tussle because his uniform was all but torn off and he had lost an eye and had to wear a patch. The captain had no choice but to make Dog stand trial along with the other sailors who had messed up on liberty that day—after all, Dog had held up the departure of the ship. As a result, Dog was restricted to the ship until the *Chaumont* reached Norfolk.

We continued through the locks and were finally back in the open sea. The *Chaumont* chugged along at her snail's pace up the coast toward Norfolk, Virginia. I had never been in the South, so I didn't know what to expect. Our drillmaster in San Diego had told us to watch our step because Norfolk was a rough place for sailors. The young civilians didn't mind messing you up, and there was almost no law and order in the black community. This proved to be true. The only time the white cops came to the black side of Norfolk was when they wanted to have some fun whipping on black heads.

Finally we arrived in Norfolk late in the evening. A Navy bus took us to the base and delivered us to where we would be quartered, Unit K West.

pieces 9

UNIT K WEST

We twenty-six sailors had our hammocks and everything we owned on our shoulders as we were led into the long barracks. I was still only one hundred and fifty pounds, the smallest guy in our group, so I guess that's why one of the guys who was there before us called to me with a greeting I had never heard before: "How's your ole black mamma?" I dropped all my gear, grabbed him, pulled him down, and started pounding on him. I was like a steel spring from all that work in the CCC and my stay with the Logginses back in Denver. Someone pulled me off and explained that he was only playing "The Dozens." That was my first introduction to The Dozens, a game played between black folks that involved a verbal put-down of your family or friends, mostly about your mamma. The insults usually went back and forth ten or twelve times until someone made that ultimate mamma insult. You had to watch out because if you laughed at anybody playing, you were in it. But the word got out: "He don't play!" I learned that some of the guys were masters at playing the game, but I didn't like it and stayed away from it.

The next morning I noticed that Unit K West was the only place on the base with a ten-foot fence around it and a little house at the entrance where we were required to sign in and out. The white boys were in a nice brick barracks and could come and go as they pleased. The only place we could go independently was the PX, a little room they had built for us attached to the main PX. In it there was a window to the main PX, where they had a jukebox, hot dogs, hamburgers, a soda fountain, pool tables, and a small store where the white boys could buy watches, razors, souvenirs, and such. We had a raggedy pool table, and if we wanted something from the other side we would have to ring a bell at the window. Sometimes they would come and ask, "What you want, boy?" but most of the time we were ignored.

Each evening, if we wanted to see the movie they played, we were marched there and put in the balcony, which was so close to the screen we had to look down. If there were not enough seats for the white boys they had our leader make us get up and march back to the barracks. Some of us didn't like what was going on, but many seemed to think that was the way we were supposed to be treated.

The white boys were drilled on pavement, while the blacks were drilled in a field with rocks and dirt clods. Since we from California had been through all the drilling before, we probably knew more about marching than the stewards who were now instructing us, so they decided to give us other jobs. I wound up running the "lucky bag." Each morning I went through the barracks, and any clothes or other articles I found lying around were taken to the lucky bag, a small room to which only I had the key. I would read the name off the item and write it on a list. The owner had to do extra duty or some other punishment to have his item returned. I also issued all the materials used for cleaning up, like soap, brass polish, and steel wool. Many of the sailors started to call me "Lucky Bag Clark," a name I still hear now and then, even after all these years. It was a way to distinguish me from the other sailors named Clark who came along at about the same time. One was Mammy Clark, and another was Funky Clark, who had a hard time keeping clean.

After three months at Unit K West the orders came to distribute us throughout the fleet. I had orders to go to work at the Naval Academy in Annapolis, Maryland, but I was sick the day I was suppose to go. They took my name off the list; it was probably the best thing that ever happened to me. When I got out of sick bay they assigned me to work at the Officers' Club on the base. My job was to serve tables at noon, then clean up. On Saturday afternoons and evenings I had to serve officers at their parties. The officers, if they felt generous, would leave maybe a dime or so as a tip, but they were very verbal with their orders as to what they wanted—"Boy, come here," and "Boy, do this," and "Boy, do that."By evening, I was

Typical "Juke Joint." They seem to be the same all over the world. (Painting by the author.)

ready to go over to Norfolk. I had formed some friendships there, and I would go down to Church Street and mingle with the other sailors and the girls who followed them. There was Battleship Margaret, Chow Chow, and Sailor Killin' Mable. Those were the names the sailors had given the young girls, and they carried them with honor. They could be trusted, and if anything came down, they were with us. Believe me, some of them could stand up and fight any sailor, and if it came down to it, they could and would pull their switchblade out of the top of their stocking. They took care of us and we them. If they were hungry, we would take them to the Chinaman's and buy them a big bowl of "Yok a Min"—nobody knew what was in it, but it would tide them over until the sailors came back the next evening.

Sometimes we took a gallon of wine up to Mable's place. The girls would turn on the phonograph, and the party would be on. I had never seen dancing like that in all my life. Those girls would move to the Huckle Buck and all the popular records of the time. You could hear their feet talking to the floor as they kept time. I was a looker and listener because I was a poor dancer.

As I look back at those girls now, I see that they were desperate young ladies just trying to make it. Even now I often think of all the respect those girls had for us and the respect we had for them.

Church Street was just as rough as they had told us it would be before we left San Diego. The street was cobblestone, and the people were so poor they were barely making it. Many of the residences had no running water or indoor plumbing, so while out walking, you had to stay in the middle of the street or else someone might suddenly yell, "Look out!" and throw the contents of their slop jar out the window and onto your head.

Finally, after about six months, my next set of orders came. Eureka! I was going back to California. I had been assigned to duty on the USS *Langley*. The *Langley* was to be stationed in San Diego, California, but for now she was at the Mare Island Naval Shipyard near San Francisco being changed from the first aircraft carrier the Navy ever had to a seaplane tender. I left Norfolk on the same old smelly ship, the *Chaumont*. We sailed down the East Coast, through Panama again to the Pacific, and up the West Coast to San Francisco. I would go aboard the *Langley* feeling assured this time—I was an old salt now.

pieces 10

USS Langley

I now felt I had reached the reason the Navy had recruited me. The anxiety was overwhelming. I was the only one from my group who had been assigned to the *Langley*. I was greeted warmly by the other mess attendants. There were some Filipino mess attendants aboard, but they were encouraged by the stewards in charge (who were almost all Filipinos) and the white officers to stay away from us black mess attendants. Divide and conquer was the order of the day. Many of the senior Filipinos were as bigoted as the white officers and mistreated us the same way. It was apparent that they wanted to maintain the status quo.

The steward in charge on the *Langley* ordered the head boy, a young black man from Indianapolis named Butler, to give me a short tour of the part of the ship where I was to work and a brief job description. As head boy, Butler's job was to help the steward carry out his orders. Butler told me the steward in charge made up all the menus, bought all the food, and was responsible for the cooks and mess attendants. He said I would be assigned to two officers. I was to shine their shoes, which they put in front of their doors each evening, take their dirty clothes to the laundry each Monday, keep their rooms clean, and be ready to greet them in the morning with a smile and ask what they wanted for breakfast. Butler looked at me and said, "I don't think they'll get many smiles out of you. Just do your job, and you'll be okay."

I was to serve lunch and dinner along with the other mess attendants. The meals were served off of silver platters, and the officers ate at tables with linen napkins and tablecloths. The mess attendants ate the same food as the officers after they were done serving them. I told Butler, "I don't like the idea of being a servant, but there's nothing I can do about it. As long as these officers respect me, I will do the best job I can." He said, "If there's anything I can help you with, let me know."

Butler had a master's degree, but here he was shining shoes, making up beds, and serving the officers. He also had an officer he was teaching college mathematics to each evening. I often wonder what happened to him, because we got split up later. We used to go on liberty together quite often. I liked the fact that neither he nor I drank, and we liked to go places where we could learn something—museums, Coit Tower, the Marina, Fisherman's Wharf. A couple of times we went over the Golden Gate Bridge to Sausalito. We had never seen ferry boats before, and they plied the San Francisco Bay by the dozen. We would ride them because we decided it was a good way to meet girls.

A few of the mess attendants stopped at the first dive on the waterfront so they could raise hell with the sailor girls. Most didn't learn anything about the customs, the people, or the country—all they knew about were the dive places. I went to some of those places sometimes, but I always wanted to see what was over the next hill. The first two officers I was assigned to as mess attendant were pleasant enough and seemed to respect me. That made my job bearable. I had already decided I would do all I could to get along, but I was not going to be abused without letting someone know how I felt about it.

The bad times came sooner than I had expected. I was sent to work in the warrant officers' mess on the ship. We only had about fifteen warrant officers, and I was unlucky enough to be assigned to Officer Diderson. He was the kind of racist bigot you see in your worst nightmares. I had been on my new assignment about a week when Diderson approached me one day. He sneered, "I can tell you're a little different than these other boys. You don't smile much and you talk like a white Yankee. I bet you think like a white boy also, don't you."

I looked him straight in the eye and responded, "I think like me."

This ship the USS *Langley* was the first Aircraft Carrier the Navy had. At the time of this picture, 1937, she had been converted to a seaplane tender.

Diderson said, "You know, I don't like niggers and I never will. I'm gonna tell you this: you better go down there and talk to some of those niggers and learn to be one if you want to get along in this Navy."

Still looking him straight in the eye, I said, "Bullshit!"

Diderson spun around, bounded up the ladder, and the next thing I knew the master-at-arms told me I was on report. I went before Captain Douglas the next morning. Diderson stood before the captain and told him, "This mess boy cursed at me, and frankly I'm scared of him."

Captain Douglas gave me a chance to explain, but he told me I should not have cursed, that there were other avenues available, though nobody had told me what they were. The captain sentenced me to the brig for three days so I would have time to "think about" what I had done.

The brig was about two decks down in the ship's bowels, where there was nothing but storerooms. My cell was four by eight feet. I was escorted out three times a day. When the escort came to my cell in the morning, I had to remove my bedding and place it outside my cell; then I was escorted to the head to wash up and use the facilities. After that I was marched to the galley, where I was issued two slices of bread and a glass of water. Then I was taken back to the brig, where I had the pleasure of sitting on the cold steel deck until noon, when the same thing happened again: two slices of bread and water. Then the same thing that evening.

After the evening ritual I could put my thin mattress back down on the cell floor and cover myself with the one thin blanket they had issued me for those cold and damp nights. The lock was thrown and I was left alone down there in the total darkness until morning—no magazines, no lights, no pencil, no paper, not anything. I got so I could mentally take myself out of the darkness, out of the cold. I could be a little boy riding Percy, or walking down the street in San Diego. This went on for three days; I had two of these experiences within about six months.

I had been fairly comfortable working in the senior officers' mess. The mess attendants there were compatible with each other. We had to do many things we didn't like, but we brothers were united together and supported each other. After I was sent to the warrant officers' mess, however, I ran across the worst black man I have ever known. In my mind he was Sambo, and his mentor was none other than Warrant Officer Diderson.

Sambo would do anything against the rest of us mess attendants to please the bigoted officer in an attempt to keep in good standing with him. Even though we mess attendants were all in the same boat, there were some Sambos who still thought that type of submissiveness and betrayal was necessary to advance in the Navy, and it was unofficially encouraged in many instances.

In addition to the butt-kissing behavior, those same black folks would report every word we spoke and every move we made to the white officers in an effort to get a feather in their cap, not realizing the officers had even less respect for them as a result of their disloyalty. Many self-respecting black folks encountered hardships because of such attitudes and behavior. I think Diderson's attitude helped motivate me to go as high as a black man could go in the Navy.

In the book *Uncle Tom's Cabin* by Harriet Beecher Stowe, Sambo was a despicable character who betrayed blacks to the white man for some imaginary benefit, while the Uncle Tom character was in fact a brave and heroic figure. Yet the characters have been confused so that one uses the term "Uncle Tom" to describe the behavior of a Sambo-type individual. That would be the same as using the name of Malcolm X or Dr. Martin Luther King to describe someone who was detrimental to the progress and advancement of black people.

Diderson would place his hand on *his* Sambo's shoulder and look at me while telling this nigger joke. He would go on about how he knew this nigger preacher as a boy, and without even finishing the joke he'd watch his Sambo react in uncontrollable laughter and antics. I would say to myself, "Look at this fool. He doesn't even know what's funny and he's already on the floor!"

The next time Sambo reacted by rolling on the floor in uncontrollable laughter, I kicked him in his ass. He, weighing about two hundred pounds, jumped up to get me, and I, this one-hundred-and-forty-pound guy who could box, kicked his butt again, good. We began boxing, and I was getting the best of him when he turned and ran through the wardroom, hollering, "Mr. Diderson! Mr. Diderson!" I was right behind him, chasing him, kicking him in the ass while the officers in the wardroom fell out of their chairs laughing.

Finally the thread snapped. One day Diderson shouted at me, "Nigger, I'll kick your belligerent black ass!" I knew he wanted me to lose my cool and hit him. That way he would be free of me forever, because I would either be kicked out of the Navy or get some time in prison. So, angry as I was, I kept from letting him have the pleasure of winning. But I was so furious, everything around me looked red. I had never felt that way before and haven't since. I ran up to the captain's cabin; a marine was on guard there. I grabbed the marine, took his rifle from him, threw it away, and had that marine up in the air, shaking him.

The captain looked out to see what all the commotion was about. He knew me; he had put me in the brig enough. He rushed out, took me by the arm, and told me to calm down. He made me come into his cabin and asked his steward to give me a cup of coffee to calm me down. I watched Captain Douglas as he sat over at his desk doing some work. Every now and then he would glance over at me to see if I had calmed down.

Finally the captain, who was about six feet three inches tall, came over to the table where I was sitting. He set his hands on the table across from me and put his face a couple of inches from mine. I knew this was about as serious as it could get. The captain of a Navy ship is about one step below God. I had respect for him, though, and I knew that even though Diderson was an officer and the captain normally had to believe him over me, it was time I told Captain Douglas the truth. I began to tell him about the abuse Officer Diderson had heaped on all of us, about his Sambo, and about how he thought I deserved the most abuse because he felt I thought I was a white man. As I talked, it all spilled out. I could see the captain getting redder and redder. Finally he got up, went to the door, and told his guard, "Go find Officer Diderson and tell him to get up here on the double!"

I heard Diderson hurry up the ladder. When he saw me standing in the captain's cabin, all the blood drained from his face, and his knees began to shake. Captain Douglas asked him about some of the allegations I had made. Diderson was so scared and confused Captain Douglas caught him almost instantly in a couple of lies. Then he told me to wait outside. I have never in my life heard one officer talk to another like he did to Diderson.

"You are a despicable specimen of a man," he spat, "and when we get back to port I'm going to talk to the admiral. You have been using me to enforce your bigotry, and I don't like it one bit. I should probably put you in the brig.

"You have shown me what kind of crap you are made of," he continued. "I am going see what we can do about all this; and don't you ever bring Clark back before me as long as you are on this ship." After the captain was through dressing Diderson down, he shouted, "Get the hell out of my sight!"

When Diderson came out I was standing there smiling at him. I was all but telling him, "I've got you now, you bastard!"

I harassed him a lot for about a month. There were no fire extinguishers on the ship, but we had buckets of sand to fight small fires. I would pick up a handful of sand, go to his room when he wasn't there, and throw it in his bed under the blanket. Or I would fill a condom with water and leave it where it would break when he got into bed, then I would tell people he had wet the bed. I wouldn't obey any of his orders. After about a week of this Diderson came to me and tried to put his hand on my shoulder to tell me he was sorry and ask me to please leave him alone. He told me I was about to drive him crazy. I told him to take his damn hand off me.

The fun ran out of it after a couple of months, and I left him alone, but he walked on eggshells around me. He tried to get some sympathy from another officer named Ripley. Ripley told him, "If you treated these mess attendants as you should, you wouldn't be having all this trouble; don't bother me with your problems."

I was still having trouble with Sambo, though. We got into a fight about every two months or so. Things got worse and worse for him as I got bigger and bigger. I was working out on the ship, boxing regularly, so each time we got into a fight he knew he was going to get his butt beat.

It was summertime, and we leisurely traveled down the West Coast. Things with me were as good as could be expected now that I'd gotten Diderson off my back. I suppose some of the officers respected me more as well.

We had been at sea for two or three days when one evening it was my turn to put out the chairs for the officers to watch movies up on deck. We did that each evening when the weather was good. I brought my mattress up and placed it on deck near the officers' quarters before the movies. I wanted to be outside where it was cool because the compartment where we stayed was directly over the fire room, and inside it would get to over a hundred degrees.

After the movies, when I went to lie down and read a little, I saw my mattress had been moved. Sambo had thrown it over by the scupper, where the water had soaked it, and had taken my place. He was lying down on his own mattress with his hands behind his head.

I went straight over and began to pound on him. He wrapped his arms around me, wrestled us up, and carried me toward the side of the ship. He held my arms to keep me from boxing him. He had me wrapped so tight, all I had to fight with were my feet and legs. I knew he had planned all this; there was no one around but him and me. He had wanted to surprise and overpower me with his size advantage.

When we reached the side of the ship, he tried to throw me over, but I was lucky enough to get my legs wrapped around the iron rails that surrounded the deck. Sambo was pushing, spitting, snorting, and his eyes were bulging. He meant to get rid of my little butt once and for all. My legs lost all feeling from trying to keep hold of that iron rail. Suddenly, someone from out of the darkness grabbed Sambo by his neck and shouted, "Turn that boy loose!"

Sambo recognized Taggart, who we all called Tiger. He was one of the biggest black men I had ever seen, and he could and would throw Sambo overboard. The officers wouldn't let Tiger work around them because they were so intimidated by his size . . . and so was Sambo.

Sambo let me go. Having had so many fights with him, this fight didn't worry me too much, except it was the first one I'd lost, and it had almost cost me my butt.

pieces 11

Initiation to Shellback

It was at about this time the *Langley* received orders to go to New York for the World's Fair in 1939. The Navy had given our captain plenty time to go through Panama and up to New York, so he used that extra time to have some fun.

When a sailor crosses the equator for the first time, he moves from being a "pollywog" to a "shellback." Captain Douglas knew we had a lot of pollywogs on board who should be initiated and made shellbacks, so he altered the course of the ship to cross the equator.

We passed the "Treasure Island" of Robert Louis Stevenson's tale, then we went on down to the Galapagos Islands. We reached the islands as the giant turtles were in their mating season. As we got close to shore we saw hundreds of giant turtles all around the ship. Captain Douglas thought it would be a good idea to capture a few of them.

They lowered a couple of boats over the side; the sailors had cargo nets in the boats. When they found some giant turtles, they threw the nets over them; the turtles began to thrash around. They got tangled in the nets, and the boats towed them back to the ship, where a crane lifted them out of the water. One was about three hundred pounds, and the big one weighed over four hundred pounds. They butchered the small one and fed it to the crew. As for the big one, we filled a boat on deck with water and took the turtle all the way to New York. I saw him there about fifteen years later, at the Bronx Zoo.

The word was given over our new speaker system: "All pollywogs and shellbacks are to assemble on deck to welcome aboard the ruler of the deep, his most revered and respectable King Neptune, and his most respected Wife and Royal Baby!" As all the sailors and officers who were pollywogs gathered on deck, a platform was raised up from over the side of the ship, and there they were, the Royal Family of King Neptune.

King Neptune had a long white beard with seaweed streaming from it. Seaweed was also hanging from his head, and he held a large pitchfork. His Wife had a long white dress covered with seaweed, and her face was garishly made up. The Royal Baby was the fattest sailor they could find aboard the ship. He had on only a diaper and three black rings painted around his navel. They read the names of all the pollywogs from the ship's records.

We were marched by the Royal Cops up to the deck above. A chute had been rigged for us pollywogs to slide down. At the bottom of the chute there was a trough filled with garbage, so as we slid down the chute, we would slide directly into this garbage. The Royal Cops would pull us out and ask us why we were so filthy; and then they turned the fire hoses on us to wash us off. We were being punished for being pollywogs.

We had to crawl on our hands and knees through a line of about twenty shellbacks with paddles who took swats at our butts. They didn't play either. For the last step we were given a bucket of soap and water and told to clean up and look like shellbacks. Then, while we were all standing there naked, they proclaimed us shellbacks. We were issued certificates later. I also had to kiss the Royal Baby's navel to show allegiance to King Neptune. My butt was still stinging from those paddles. I could only hope that at some future date I would be the shellback to lay that paddle on some pollywog to get even.

The *Langley* left the West Coast and slipped into the Panama Canal. By this time I had become an old salt, so most of the excitement was gone. The brothel part of Balboa had been wiped out—Panama was trying to clean up her image—so we went on through the canal and out the Atlantic side.

Captain Douglas decided the crew of the *Langley* should learn something about countries like Haiti, Cuba, and some of the other islands in the Caribbean. I loved it; we black sailors were around people who looked like us. Unlike the civilians on cruise ships, we could go anywhere on the islands. We really wanted to go so we could see what those places were really like. Most of the people loved us; we were treated like kings.

The young people swam out to meet our ship a mile or more before we got to port. We had been told to save all the tin cans, our old clothes, and shoes to throw over the side. After gathering what they wanted, the swimmers would tie the items around their waists and swim home. Some of the sailors threw quarters overboard to the young swimmers. We could see the quarters flickering in the crystal clear water; and then a young kid would swim to the top with a coin. I had never seen anyone who could swim so long and were as agile as these young people. We could see sand sharks swimming right there beside them, so I guess they knew what they were doing and felt they were in no danger.

We stayed in Haiti for about a whole week. I will never forget the beautiful young women there; they had never seen black sailors before and were very attracted to us. Being in my twenties, I will always remember my line: "I want to take you to New York!" Shame on me. I'm sure the girls felt as bad as we did when we had to leave for New York. Haiti was a beautiful experience. All the negatives about my situation could be tolerated as long as I could have experiences like that. Life was good.

We leisurely moved up the East Coast, our top speed only slightly faster than that of the turtle we had captured in the waters around the Galapagos Islands. As we sailed north, I and many of the other sailors aboard started looking forward to the experience of going to the big city. We stopped at Norfolk, Virginia, again to let the Navy Yard look over the old bucket and spruce her up a little so when we got to New York we would look our best.

Norfolk was just as bad as it had been when we were there in the boot camp days. All the filth, rats, and cockroaches were still there, along with the hard race prejudice that we black sailors were forced to face—sitting in the back of the bus, being called "boy," and the abuse by both the black and white populations. I stayed aboard ship most of the two weeks we were there. We left with the *Langley* all painted up and looking as good as an old rusty bucket could look.

pieces 12

New York

It was a bright, beautiful evening when we finally reached New York. We arrived at our berth at the end of Manhattan Island, where we were to tie up the Old Lady. They called that area "The Battery." I will never forget the sight as I looked up at the skyscrapers, sixty or more stories tall, all cluttered together. To me it seemed like a fantasyland. It took me days to get over the awe. When I got my liberty, I left the ship and went up to Harlem.

I had a lady friend who lived in Harlem, and she told me how to get there from the ship. I left the ship in uniform and decided to stop first at a barbershop on 125th Street to get a haircut. The barber there told me, "No, I'm not going to cut your hair, 'cause you a nigga flunky." That was a beautiful welcome to New York. Then I began to hear the young kids calling to me, "Which shoe did you shine this morning, shoe-shine boy?" Some of the statements were even worse. Later I found out that some of the black organizations had started a campaign to put us down for being mess attendants in the Navy. They blamed us for the situation we were in.

I finally got to my lady friend's house, and she decided to show me Harlem. Being with a young lady friend and going to all the clubs in Harlem, the people finally let me alone. We went to the Apollo Theater, Savoy Ballroom, and all the rest. I had been seriously gambling aboard ship and had a pocketful of money. Most of the clubs were really laid out. I will never forget one club where the dancers were dressed so elegantly, and the lighting was as glamorous as the ladies were. I did not know what I was about to experience.

There were great performances, and in between each revue and dance I saw something remarkable. A male patron would put a quarter on the edge of the table, and this beautiful young dancer would glide over, guided by the music, move over the edge of the table, and the quarter would be gone, all gracefully done to the beat of the music. I had been through a lot and had seen as much, but this was fantastic. I thought I had seen it all, but to my delight the dancer moved to the center of the dance floor, still connected to the music, and gracefully dispersed the quarters. All the clubs had floor shows that included a dance review, but that act topped them all.

Harlem 1939

Getting up on Sunday morning, having some grits and eggs for breakfast. Getting the kids washed up and off to Sunday school. Older folks getting dressed, goin' to church to praise the Lord. The smell of Sunday dinner: fried chicken, collard greens, cornbread, and lemonade.

Hot summer sun beating down on the concrete in front of the brownstone houses, no grass; folks sitting, laughing, gossiping; kids playing stickball in the street.

Cool cats strutting by, swinging one arm, dragging one leg, walking cool in their zoot suits, the pants half a yard wide at the knee, so small at the bottom you couldn't hardly squeeze your foot through; coats coming down to the knee, chains swinging, big apple hats, big as a basket, fuzzy and all. Long yellow shoes. If you were carrying a horn case, you were really cool. This was the time of *hep*, not *hip* (when white folks caught on to the black slang, they changed the word to *hip*).

Joe Louis, Sugar Ray Robinson, and black poets. Tap dancers like the Nicholas Brothers, Bo Jangles Robinson, tapping up a storm to the rhythms of the great bands led by Duke Ellington, Count Basie, Fletcher Henderson, and all the rest. Great horn men like Yard Bird Parker, Illinois Jackquet, standing on the stage at the Apollo Theater in a battle of horns. One on each side of the stage, stomping those long yellow shoes to punctuate their licks.

Great Lady vocalists like Ella Fitzgerald, Sarah Vaughn, Pearl Bailey, and Lena Horn doin' their thing, and everybody diggin' it.

Nightclubs staying open all night. Those great floor shows, and ladies dance revues, and comedians like Pigmeat Markum, Redd Foxx, and others. Patrons putting quarters on the edge of tables; dancers coming to the table, squatting over it to the music, moving on, quarters gone.

Savoy Ballroom, jitterbug, men and women contorting their bodies to the beat of the music, slinging their partners in the air, through their legs, sliding them on their butts and all, zoot suits flashing, feet flying, skirts whirling, legs flashing—what a sight.

Pimps standing on corners, watching their ladies with eagle eyes. Dope sellers keeping an eye out for their customers and the law.

The A train bringing all those folks up to Harlem from Brooklyn. Ladies dressed in evening gowns and gold shoes, going to the ball with all that fried chicken in those fancy purses; men in tuxedoes going to party on Saturday and Sunday nights.

Sugar Hill, where rich whites folks once lived with elevators, doormen, maid service, and all the rest. Whites moved out, blacks moved in. Can't go to apartments or hotels downtown; it's not allowed.

Doctors, lawyers, musicians, undertakers, rich hustlers—all lived there. Rib joints, barbershops, beauty shops,

> shoe-shine stands, liquor stores—all of this and more made up Harlem.

That was my first taste of a real big city. I liked it for a while, but it soon got boring. The artificial way of living there was not all that desirable to me because I was easily satisfied by the less exotic things of life.

We were in New York about two weeks, then we left and went back down the East Coast, through the Panama Canal again, and up the West Coast to San Diego, our home port.

Once we arrived in San Diego, I began to look up some of the people I knew. I bought a 1937 Ford convertible and was really living a good life. I was transferred off the *Langley* after about two more years, when the Navy decided to send the *Langley* to the Asiatic Fleet. In those days they had a fleet of ships that stayed in the Orient. They would change personnel, but the ships stayed there. The fleet, because of all the prejudice, didn't want any of us black sailors contaminating the Asian people, so any time a ship joined the Asiatic Fleet, they took the black sailors off the ships and reassigned us.

pieces 13

Kaneohe, Hawaii

I left San Diego in 1940 to go to the new Kaneohe Navy Air Base in Hawaii. The base was right over a little mountain range that separated one side of the island from the other, with Pearl Harbor about five miles away. I was now in a seaplane squadron, VP11. I first was a butcher, then a baker, and finally a cook. We cooked for the base administration and the officers who flew the planes. By now we were working in a more relaxed atmosphere, and we got along well with the officers, but when I went to Pearl Harbor sometimes to see a movie on the base, I was reminded that the same old discrimination and race separation was alive and well.

The movies at Pearl Harbor were shown outside. The officers sat in chairs; the sailors sat on large logs in rows. There was a rope stretching across the back; the blacks had to sit behind the rope. That was Pearl Harbor in 1940.

We black sailors had our own places where we hung out in Honolulu. One was 2 Jacks, a bar on Hotel Street. The bar was owned by a black man; it was the place where many black sailors went. Dorie Miller was one of our crowd. The owner let us regulars use the private room in back, where there was a big round table that could hold a lot of people. We rolled the dice to see who was to buy the first round of drinks. Then it would go on around the table from there. Sometimes on Saturday or Sunday we stayed there all day telling stories, lying, and singing. We had some good times there.

At first we brought our girlfriends, but they always found some way to make trouble, so we agreed to bring them only on Sunday—

and only the girls who we knew would not mess up. And that didn't just apply to the women. If a sailor messed up too often, we would ban him too.

There were two dime-a-dance places on Hotel Street. The dances cost you a dime a ticket, which you gave to the girl for each dance. One place was upstairs; they played records there. The other place had live music, but it was still a dime a dance.

There was a black band that played there; Thelonius Monk was one of the musicians. I can't remember any of the others' names, but they could really jam. These were the black sailors' and soldiers' places. White boys were allowed if they behaved themselves. If they didn't show the girls respect or got too drunk, we would throw them out, and the girls would help us.

It was there that I began to wear my hair conked. The female vocalist in Thelonius Monk's band would pick up a few extra dollars by straightening our hair for some of us. All you needed was lye, potatoes, grease, and plenty of water! The water was important to kill the heat from the lye.

One day she got all the lye and such on my hair and began singing with the band while the stuff was still on. Then one of the guys playing in the band came over to me and said the water had been cut off. That stuff was burning and giving me a fit. The band had played too long, and she had sung too long. It burned my scalp so bad that the next morning my head was one big sore.

I went to the doctor and got some salve to put on it. He asked me about the sores. I got cold feet and was too ashamed to tell him the truth. Soon he had the laboratory taking cultures and everything else to find out what the strange disease was. Then he quarantined me and told me I couldn't work around food. By then it had gone on too long to tell him the truth. I felt like a fool. After about a week I began to heal. Finally he let me go back to work, still baffled by the strange thing that had happened to me.

My commanding officer had an inspection soon after. The whole squadron was there. As the captain moved up and down the ranks, inspecting the sailors, he turned to his yeoman and told him to keep all the stewards behind when inspection was over; he wanted to talk to the black sailors. There were about six or eight of us. When he came back to talk to us, the first words from his mouth were, "I want you men to think about this: you don't have to put all that lye, potato, and lard in your hair to make it straight. Have pride in yourselves and wear your hair the way God made it."

I thought, Wow, this coming from a white man from Virginia. He even knows how to make it!

Just as I was thinking that he said, "I know how to make that conk, and I know how to put it in your hair. You don't need it!"

He couldn't have said anything to make me have more respect for him. I was with him for about two years after that, and I never conked my hair again.

Time passed. I was gambling again, making money hand over fist and spending it just as fast. I now had an apartment off base in Honolulu with a fully stocked bar and a lot of girls, and I owned a car. Life was good for me until Sunday, December 7, 1941.

I was on duty that beautiful Sunday morning, in my room on the base, which was in the same building where the officers slept. It was my duty as telephone watchman to call the officers to the phone if they received a call. It had been quiet that morning until about eight o'clock. I heard planes flying over the building and wondered why they were coming in so low.

I got out of bed and was sitting on the side putting my shoes on when I heard machine gun fire. At that moment a round came through my window. The bullet went through my mattress about a foot from me, bounced around my room, which was made of concrete, and lodged in a chair near me. I ran outside and looked up and saw all these planes flying over—Japanese planes. I ran inside to try to get the officers up. Most thought I was crazy and ignored me initially, but it didn't take long for them to realize it was the real thing.

The planes flew in a large circle over the BOQ (bachelor officers' quarters) before strafing all the brand-new planes sitting on the runway, planes our squadron had brought to the base only two weeks before. The Japanese planes were only about fifty feet up; we could see the pilots' faces. One plane had two cockpits. There was a gunner standing up in the rear cockpit with a machine gun. As they flew over he saw all us black sailors down on the loading dock. I looked at him and he grinned and waved at us—I will never forget that look.

The next pass over I think he decided to have some fun, because as the pilot swung around, the gunner pointed his machine gun at us. He didn't fire. He could have killed us all. We all ran toward the building and tried to rush through the door at the same time, getting jammed in the doorway. We all seemed to look up at the same time and see as the Japanese pilot just laughed and flew on.

The base had no defense. Down at the galley, the sailors were throwing rocks and potatoes at the planes as they flew over. The Japanese burned up all of our pretty new planes, then for good measure they dropped two or three bombs. After that they got back into formation and flew away. We could see all the planes burning and could see the smoke coming over the hill from Pearl Harbor.

At about that time a sailor drove up in a Navy pickup truck loaded with rifles and ammunition. The Filipino steward in charge told me, "Clark, you are the sergeant. Issue these rifles to all the boys and establish a beachhead down on the beach," which was about fifty yards away from the BOQ, past some tall weeds and a couple of trees.

The Navy at this time hadn't taught us anything about guns. We opened the cases of rifles and found they were packed full of a very thick grease that had to be removed before the rifles could be fired. None of us knew how to clean that stuff out of the guns, so we got sticks and such to try to get it out. I'm sure glad we didn't try to fire them because they probably would have blown our heads off. I told my men, the mess attendants, to stuff all their pockets full of bullets. Then I realized we had only white uniforms to wear. I put about five pounds of coffee in a bag and made a large pot of coffee in one of the steam kettles and had each of the guys throw a uniform and a hat into the pot. We boiled them for about twenty minutes to turn them brown.

I opened the fridge so they could get some bread and bologna to eat because we didn't know how long we would be out there. Then I stationed them along the beach. I told them not to move after dark and to shoot anything that moved. The moon shone bright as we lay in those weeds, about fifty of us, all scared as hell. There were all

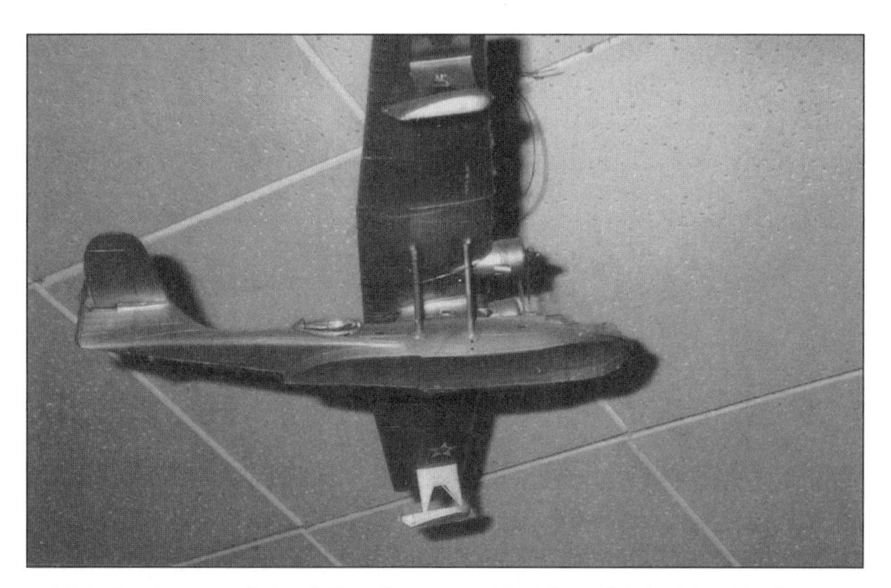

This is the model of the famous PBY, in which Mr. Clark, as steward, had logged thousands of miles with the Commander of Squadron VP11. On Dec. 7, 1941 during the bombing of Kaneohe Bay, his squadron lost all the new planes on the ground.

sorts of rumors coming back to me that the Japanese had landed and so on. We didn't know what to believe.

We were never so glad to see the sun come up. We were greeted by one of our planes diving on a small two-man submarine right in front of the beach where we had been all night. About ten o'clock or so the word got to me to have all the boys bring the rifles and ammunition up to the BOQ and throw them back onto the Navy pickup truck. The white sailor in the truck told me, "We'll fight this war." I thought, This is the way you think—you wanted us yesterday to help save your butt; today you say you don't need us and want us to get out of your face.

Navy intelligence had found that the Japanese fleet had turned around, so now we were not in immediate danger. We cleaned up and went back to our jobs as usual—I to the galley to cook, the other mess attendants to their jobs of taking care of the white officers.

At the time the Japanese-American battalion stationed in

Honolulu controlled most of the roads and everything else, but that would soon change as paranoia caused by the attack increased. The marines came to our barracks that second night, when the base was blacked out in case of a second attack. They made a raid on our quarters, forcing us to open our lockers as if we were the enemy. They had rifles with fixed bayonets. They pulled our belongings out of our lockers and trampled over our clothes, cameras, and other personal items with their combat boots, probing in the dark with their flashlights, treating us like dogs.

The next morning my partner Lyles and I went down to the galley to cook breakfast. There was a marine standing at the end of the galley at parade rest with a fixed bayonet on his rifle, watching us cook.

I asked Lyles, "Hey, man, what do you think about this crap? They stomped all over our stuff last night, and today they're treating us like we're the enemy. What could that bastard do if we wanted to do something to this damn food? Somebody is just plain stupid."

It so happened I knew the marine colonel who was in charge, so when we got through cooking breakfast, I asked Lyles if he would go with me and tell the colonel about the marine in the galley. I didn't think he would have ordered this and figured he probably didn't even know about it.

"D-d-damn right," Lyles responded. "I'll g-go with you. W-w-what're we going to say?" He was stuttering now, so I knew he was excited.

"Don't worry, the colonel knows me, and I think he's an all-right guy."

We went down to his office. He saw me outside and told me to come in. I guess he could see we were upset. I asked him, "Colonel, do you know there's a marine standing at parade rest in our galley, watching us cook?"

He said, "No, I didn't know that, but by the time you get back he'll be gone!"

The marine *was* gone when we returned. I wanted to tell the colonel about the raid the night before, but I thought I'd better stop while I was ahead.

After the attack on Pearl Harbor, Hawaii was never the same. Before Pearl Harbor, the Hawaiian people and the Japanese-Americans, who made up seventy-five percent of the population, mostly controlled Hawaii. Black folks were treated with respect then, and it was a wonderful place for us to live. The police chief and most of the police force were Hawaiian and Japanese, with a few Filipinos. The women considered it an honor to be a part of the culture of color. But the war changed all that. The Americans, mostly the southern ones (who were the majority of the military), considered all those who were not white a lower class of people, so now many of the Samoans, Tongans, and Japanese-Americans were considered inferior.

The families of the officers in my squadron who had occupied Navy houses on the base were sent back to the States shortly after the Japanese attack. Now they used the quarters to house the Navy officers. The captain's house was big enough for four officers. A small room that had previously been the maid's quarters now housed myself and King Jinks, my assistant (yes, that was really his name). My responsibilities were to run the house, do the cooking, and buy the supplies. This turned out to be one of the best times in the Navy for me. We lived there as one big happy family. I did the best I could with supplies being so low; no one ever complained. The captain flew over to another island a couple of times to get beef, which tasted like heaven to all of us. We had some good little dinner parties and barbecues.

At one dinner party the captain invited a doctor and his wife. I cooked roast beef, mashed potatoes, and gravy. Me and King Jinks were passing the food around on trays to the officers and their guests. The doctor's wife was telling a story and waving her hands to make a point. Well, just as I started to lower the tray of potatoes and gravy, her hand hit it. The gravy went up in the air and landed in her ample bosom. I, flustered about the whole thing, reached down the front of her dress to retrieve the gravy ladle. By this time the captain was laughing so hard, the lady's husband pushed him, knocked him over, and the lady was fighting me because I had put my hand down her dress. Meanwhile, the rest of the officers were laughing, or trying not to.

Finally, after everything had settled down and she had cleaned all the gravy and potatoes off herself, everybody began to laugh; it got so funny she wrote a poem about it. And every time she came to dinner, when I got around to serve her she would freeze and say something funny.

pieces 14

Guadalcanal

The war was raging farther down in the South Pacific. The Marines and Army had invaded Guadalcanal, and now the island was secured. They needed a system of support so they could move up through the islands. Guadalcanal, an island among a group known as the Solomon Islands, was to become a staging area and support base for the offensive.

In 1942 my squadron was ordered to Guadalcanal. The Navy had formed PATSU 1-3, which was made up of several of the patrol squadrons combined, including mine, VP11. When we got there we learned we had to cut out a piece of jungle and set up a base where the officers and men could operate our planes. By that time I had advanced to chief steward. The only thing about the promotion similar to the white chiefs was that we made the same amount of money. I was prohibited from sleeping in the normal chiefs' quarters and was prevented from social contact with them, nor could I eat in the chiefs' mess. I had to sleep and eat with the regular sailors. While the CBs (construction battalions) got the base ready, Captain Clark put me in charge of a makeshift baking operation we had set up. It was unheard of for a black man to be put in charge of whites in the Navy—or anywhere else—in 1942, but my commanding officer was in charge of the twenty or so white sailors, so there was nothing anyone could do about it. I got along with all of them pretty well, except one young sailor from Tennessee named Jenkins.

One day, as he was mixing a batch of dough for some bread, I noticed he was crying. I asked him what was wrong. He told me his daddy had taught him all his life to hate niggers, and if his daddy knew he was working for a nigger, he would probably kill himself. I told him, "Come to my tent this evening after work; I want to talk to you."

At about six o'clock Jenkins arrived outside my tent.

"Come on in," I said.

Jenkins hesitated.

"Come on in," I repeated.

He reluctantly entered, and I offered him a seat. I told him to get all he was feeling off his chest.

"Like I said, I just don't like you people."

I thought, This is good; at least he didn't call me a nigger this time.

I explained that I didn't feel the same anger toward him, though I had a reason to. "So," I continued, "how can you hate me for no reason at all? You might not realize how much of a load you are carrying around with all that anger toward me. All I ask of you is that you do your job and everything will be okay."

Jenkins seemed to accept my advice and became the most reliable man in my crew. I complimented him when he did a good job; he began to talk to me with respect. I felt good for him. He seemed to be letting go of his senseless anger toward black folks; I hoped so. By the time I left Guadalcanal he told me that he loved me more than his daddy and that he would never go back to Tennessee.

The CBs had built us a brick oven about twelve feet long, and we made bread for the whole island at first, about seven hundred loaves a day. We had to go to the abandoned supply dump for flour, shortening, and so on. All the flour was loaded with weevils by that time. At first we tried to sift the weevils out, but it took too much time, so we made the bread, weevils and all. The Army had some butter that you could not melt on the stove, but you could spread it on that bread, and the fellas loved it. Then we got some new flour without weevils and used it. Some of the guys started complaining. "What happened to the good bread?" We didn't tell them.

I ran the bakery for about two months; once the CBs built the officers' mess, I ran that for the remainder of the year. I had only three kinds of meat to use in my menus. One time they brought us some lamb, and another time I was lucky to get hold of some turkeys and hams. But other than those two times, all I had to use for my menus were Spam, Vienna sausage, and corned beef.

I had to go down to an old abandoned food dump to get everything I used. The pile of stuff there was about as high as a house. All the sugar sacks had rotted, so when we went digging through the dump to see what we could find, we had to fight off big black ants that were about half an inch long. We'd find canned beans, canned corn, canned peas—even canned butter. The butter had been prepared so it could not melt. You could put it on the stove and it would not melt. The flour and coffee were in five-gallon cans, shortening also.

That year I think I did everything with Spam and Vienna sausage but serve it as dessert. I breaded it, chopped it, made soup out of it and sandwich spread. I got the reputation of having the best food on Guadalcanal, and I have a commendation to prove it.

At Christmastime I heard about some ships down in Espíritu Santo that had all kinds of fresh goodies. Espíritu Santo was an island about five hundred miles south of Guadalcanal where all kinds of supply ships came and distributed supplies throughout the South Pacific. I talked my captain into flying me down to check it out. Sure enough, one of the ships had turkeys, cranberries, hams, fresh apples and oranges, and Christmas candy. I got two dozen turkeys, some hams, and everything else they had.

On Christmas Eve we stayed up all night cooking those turkeys on Army field ranges—we could only cook four at a time. The officers knew we were preparing a feast, so they decorated the mess hall. They put up some kind of bush for a Christmas tree, decorated the tables with flowers from the surrounding jungle, made a Merry Christmas banner, and even rehearsed a couple of songs.

On Christmas Day we served all those fat turkeys, one on each table. We decided to leave the carving to them. We also had cranberry sauce, fresh frozen peas, gravy, and candied sweet potatoes. The officers brought their own assortment of homemade wine and rotgut, and a few had real whiskey. They celebrated for about two hours, then they began to chant, "Clark! Clark! Clark!" I was staying in the background, but they came out and got me and hoisted me over their heads as they stomped, clapped, and gave me a great ovation that I will never forget.

One of the first things I did when I got to Guadalcanal was to buy me a jeep. The soldiers were selling them to what they called tourists—us—for fifty bucks. You could buy a four-by-four truck for a hundred bucks. The jeep gave me some mobility so I could visit other units to gamble and could follow the good movies when they came. I saw *Cabin in the Sky* about a dozen times, driving from one camp to another, as well as some of the other black movies that were released during that era.

One of my men, Bayle, decided he needed transportation too and bought a four-by-four truck from the solders instead of a jeep. One day a ship came in with a load of beer and liquor for the troops. It anchored a short distance from the island, and boats loaded with the cargo made their way to the beach. The Army had a line of trucks ready to receive the cargo. Bayle got in line too with his Army truck. They loaded about two hundred cases of beer and some liquor on his truck. Instead of taking his load to the warehouse, he hid it someplace in the jungle and sold the beer for fifty dollars a case. Liquor was a hundred bucks a quart. He made a bundle; many servicemen got rich down there.

Another of my men had a still; there were many on the island. One of his customers was Admiral Halsey when he came to the island. Later his still blew up, sending mash and raisins all over the high command quarters. He never heard anything about it.

At least twice that I can recall, one of the enterprising officers brought a couple of Navy nurses to camp. They stayed about two days and left rich—two hundred bucks a whack. I was glad when they left. Those officers were drinking and fighting and raising Cain over them for the whole two days.

We had one steward who decided to build himself a boat. He worked on that little boat the whole year, on his own time. It was only about eight feet long, the boards going in all directions. He had to tell you what it was before you could recognize it. He went about it quietly every day, changing things as he went along. Now I understand what he was doing; he only wanted to do something to make his time pass more rapidly. He knew the junk would never float.

Although we were on Guadalcanal, all those miles from the States, sloshing around in the rain and mud during monsoon season, "Tokyo Rose" was beaming us the latest and best music from Tokyo. Sometimes she would direct her comments at us black servicemen. She would say, "Jim, I hope you like this new song by Duke Ellington, and I hope Jody isn't successful in his attempt to take your girl from you there in L.A. You could be dancing with her or having a tender moment with her right now! Think about it. I can't understand why you are there in all that mud and rain anyway; you know how that white man hates you back home. Well, Jim, this is for you, "Sophisticated Laadeee," by Duke Ellington. . . . Bye, Jim."

For a while the Japanese bombers—which we called Mitsubishis because they were made by the Mitsubishi Company—flew over each night and dropped a few bombs. They rarely hit anything. They were mainly doing it to keep us awake—harassment bombing would be the best way to describe it. We referred to them as Washing Machine Charlie because of the almost rhythmic drone of their engines. When the air raid siren sounded, we would jump out from under the mosquito nets over our cots and dive into the bomb shelters. Those mosquitoes seemed as big as horses and would always get us while we waited in the bomb shelters. After the bombers were gone we would go back to our tents, slip under the mosquito nets, and hope we could sleep the rest of the night. At the time, I never thought I would have a Mitsubishi TV in my house and rent one of their cars, as I did on my last vacation.

One day four P-38s blazed in onto our airstrip. They were the hottest planes we had at that time. The pilots were Army Air Force, but they were dressed in all black, with black cowboy hats, and each had two silver-plated .45s. Their planes were also painted black. They told us they were Night Fighters. Their job was to stop the Mitsubishis from harassing us each night. Sure as hell, that night, when they thought the planes were on the way, they flew up higher than the planes would be coming in and waited. We all knew what would happen. Pretty soon we heard Washing Machine Charlie, then the Night Fighters dropped down from above. We could see the tracer bullets from the ground. It took about two minutes before we saw that bomber shot out of the sky. That was the last of the harassment from Washing Machine Charlie.

We black sailors stayed about a hundred yards from where the white sailors lived in their Quonset huts. One of those sailors owned a small female monkey. Each day when the sailor went to work the monkey came over to where all us black guys were. I would watch her as she walked a few feet on her hind legs, then jumped up in the tall grass to see if she was going the right way. When she got to the barracks where the black guys stayed, she pushed the screen door all the way open because she knew a rubber band would close it fast. She would jump in and the door would just miss her tail, then she would stand and look around to see who was there. She would approach and choose one of us to climb on. When she made her choice, it was better to leave her alone, because if you didn't she would bite you. About dark she would decide to go home. She would go to the door, look back, and talk monkey talk as if to say, "Let me out." I would watch as her little head bobbed up and down as she made her way home in the tall grass.

Mahogany trees were everywhere on the island. Most were hollow at the bottom; the cavity went up inside the trees thirty feet or more. In the daytime, if you looked up there, it was black with the bats that came out at night. The iguanas and coconut crabs also slept in the daytime, but at night those crabs would be seen standing a foot or so tall, with claws as large as a person's hand. They could pinch your fingers off they were so powerful. Most of us went barefoot when we first got there until we learned we could get jungle rot. It put me in the hospital for awhile. There were no women on the island (the US had moved them all by the time I got there), no stores, no nothing. I was there a whole year doing the monotonous job of feeding the officers.

The English who had colonized Guadalcanal before the war had converted its people to Christianity and put them to work raising coconuts. The natives were black as coal and had fuzzy hair, and the English had given them the name Fuzzy Wuzzees. They had been cannibals and headhunters until the early 1900s, and many of the old men were still around from those days. One old fellow used to come to visit me. He still had the hash marks on his arm to show how many men he had killed.

The chief, even during the war, had a way of reminding all he was still chief. He would have his men get his dugout canoe, which was made from a giant mahogany tree. There was a high seat in the back where he sat in all his plumage, with war paint on his face. About a dozen of his men paddled the boat around the island, singing a cadence as they paddled. The natives would be down at the beach waving and showing their respect.

On Sunday the chaplain had church. The congregation sat on logs. Many of the natives would come, but they were required to stand in back. The young men would be there with their chests bare, cloth wrapped around their waists, and large wooden combs in their hair. None of them had shoes. The armed forces did not have shoes large enough for them. Those who were ready to be married had their hair dyed flaming red. They dyed it with betel nut, and the natives also chewed it. It was a mild narcotic.

My year was finally up on Guadalcanal. I was about to be sent back to the States for a thirty-day leave. Warrant Officer Gossick told me he would take me down to catch a transport ship to take me back to San Francisco. The anxiety was almost overwhelming in the weeks before leaving. I was so sick of that place. The day I was to leave, I saw that big old country boy from Tennessee who had called me a nigger a year before. He came to me and told me, "I want to carry your bags, because you opened my eyes, and now I have gotten rid of all that hate my daddy put into me." So off we went to catch the Norwegian ship that was being used to transport US military personnel back to the States. I'd been away for about three years altogether.

pieces 15

Back to the States

The ship took about fifteen days to reach San Francisco. It was cold and foggy that morning as we passed under the Golden Gate Bridge. I had been under her many times before, but that morning she was the most beautiful I had ever seen.

We were loaded onto buses and taken to Treasure Island. Some large buildings from the 1939 World's Fair had been converted into barracks for the sailors and marines coming from and going to the

This was our first night in States after three years in the South Pacific, 1943. I'm second from the right.

war, which was still raging in the Pacific.

I hadn't realized how much the States had changed since I left three years ago, before the war started. There was military activity everywhere—war plants, shipyards, uniformed men and women. It was the first time I had been in contact with sailors who were not mess attendants or stewards. I felt very pleased that black people were at last given a choice of jobs in the Navy.

We arrived in San Francisco on a Saturday, and I had permission to go on my thirty-day leave on Sunday. I had about five thousand dollars in my money belt as I caught a train to Denver to see my brother Kenneth. I hadn't seen Kenneth since leaving Denver to join the Navy, and I had not seen Keith, my youngest brother, since he came to see me at the Logginses in East Lake, Colorado, when I was about fourteen years old. I was hoping to see him also, but I did not get the opportunity.

After spending a week with Kenneth, I then went on to Washington, DC, where Katherine and Korea were living. I hadn't seen Katherine since she was about nine or Korea since she was about seven. They were both in their twenties now. When I arrived they were at work. I left a note, not telling them who it was from, but they knew my handwriting. I waited next door for them to come home. About six or so I went back to their apartment. The door was open, and I watched as Katherine tidied up the place. I didn't even know which of my sisters she was when she asked me, "Which one am I?" That really made me realize just how much of their lives I had missed out on. So we tried to make it all up in the short time we had. Five young ladies were staying in the same apartment as my sisters. When they all got home, the party was on. We partied for the two or so weeks I was there, and I do mean party. I'll never forget what a good time we had.

Regrettably, the time came for me to get back to San Francisco so I could be reassigned. When I left there were three cabs full of ladies to see me off. It was a miracle that I did finally leave. As I headed back to San Francisco, I felt as though I would be assigned somewhere in the South Pacific, or on a ship going there. I could only think about the fact that I had two more weeks in San Francisco before being reassigned. I still had plenty of money, so I thought, What the hell; I'll probably get killed anyway, so let the good times roll.

My wife Flo was a professional entertainer. Here she is at the piano. She has been a great influence on my life.

One night I walked into Slim Jenkins, a nightclub in Oakland, and *wow!* There was this beautiful fox playing the piano. Shipyard workers were trying to talk trash to her and stuffing bills into the kitty on the piano. I held up a ten so everyone could see and stuffed it in that kitty's mouth and said, "I'll see you later." Damned if she didn't tell all those guys no and say, "This is my friend." Her name was Florence; I called her Flo. And from that we were married two weeks later.

pieces 16

The Aaron Ward

Right about that time my orders came and I was assigned to a ship, so I knew it would not be long before I was back in the war. The only good thing about the assignment was the ship, the USS *Aaron Ward*, which was a brand-new destroyer. That meant a whole new crew would have to be assigned and trained, so it would be at least four or five months before we were ready to go. The Navy was desperately in need of destroyers. Our ships were small and fast and were expected to stand up to almost any situation—we were also considered expendable. This was serious now, no more playing around.

The Navy had a core of seasoned sailors, like myself, to train the new kids. By that time I had been in the Navy about eight years. I was assigned five mess attendants to train to take care of the officers, and I was to run the officers' mess.

I had one cook, Eurice, who had been a chef at the St. Francis Hotel in San Francisco. He was an excellent cook, but at first he got seasick every time the ship sailed. That meant I had to cook in his place for two or three days each time we left port until Eurice came out of his hole and reassumed his duties.

We were training the new crew in different phases, sailing up and down the coast as different stages of the training progressed. The Navy referred to it as a shakedown cruise. Flo moved up and down the coast also so that we could spend as much time together as possible. It was particularly rough for us since we had only been married about six months; we hardly knew each other. While we

Brand new out of the shipyard, the *Aaron Ward* was camouflaged for visual protection. The camouflage, however was removed before she set sail. 1943.

were conducting our shakedown cruise, the Allied forces landed in Normandy, the first step in liberating Europe from the grasp of the Nazi occupation.

Eventually we finished our training. I had been sent to gunnery school and firefighting school. When the ship was in combat, my military battle station was to put out fires and, if need be, take a job on one of the forty-millimeter anti-aircraft guns. Our skipper was Captain Sanders; he was a beautiful person, and the crew loved him. Captain Sanders called all the crew on deck and announced that the *Ward* and the crew were ready to join the fleet. He asked us, "Are you ready to fight the enemy?" At that point all those young, pink-faced kids to whom this must have seemed like a movie threw their hats in the air and cheered and stomped their feet. I thought, They will soon change their tune when the bombs begin to fall and they begin to see their shipmates splattered all over the deck.

Finally it came time for the ship to take on ammunition. We were sent to Port Chicago in California. All the sailors I saw driving ammo trucks and handling the ammo were black. I thought it fit the pattern. All my messmen had been assigned to the ammunition magazines aboard ship, which was one of the most hazardous jobs, and at Port Chicago all the black men had deliberately been assigned to the most hazardous job there. Two weeks after the *Aaron Ward* was serviced at Port Chicago, an explosion occurred and 320 men were killed. 202 were black sailors. Those who remained refused to work under such conditions and 50 blacks were court-martialed for mutiny. Some were sent to prison; others were given a dishonorable discharge, which followed them throughout the rest of their lives.

pieces 17

The South Pacific

We left California to join the fleet somewhere near the China Sea. It took us about two weeks to get to the South Pacific Theater. We were to escort the fleet while they performed maneuvers and guard the larger ships, like the aircraft carriers, troop transports, and utility ships. The *Aaron Ward*, like all destroyers, was fast and highly maneuverable. If submarines attacked the fleet, we were to hunt them down and destroy them with our depth charges. We were there to shoot down enemy aircraft and form an outer perimeter around the fleet, placing ourselves in the way of torpedoes or any other threats—after all, that's what being expendable meant.

After several months of fleet-escort duty, our mission changed. Up to that point our tour of duty had been pretty much uneventful, but now our forces were about to invade the island of Okinawa. The assignment: help sweep mines from around the island to make it safer for the incoming ships carrying our soldiers and marines.

We spent about two weeks minesweeping before the invasion. During that time, I was on deck once when we came across an unusual-looking object bobbing in the water just ahead of us. It was half a human body floating in the calm sea, undoubtedly the remains of a Japanese pilot. The body was cut off at the waist, the flight jacket still on. I wondered if he had lost his legs in the crash or if the sharks got them.

Our ship stopped, and one of our sailors used a grappling hook to hoist the body aboard. A number of us sailors stood there gaping.

Then someone unbuttoned one of the pockets on the jacket and removed a small leather folder. In it were some papers and a picture of a young Japanese woman and two beautiful, smiling children. After removing this from the jacket, the sailor disdainfully kicked the body back into the sea.

That was the first time any of the war stuff got to me. A strange feeling came over me, and I remember saying a small prayer to myself: "Please, God, stop this killing." Even though I had not had any direct involvement in pulling the body from its tomb, I felt guilty, as though his blood was on my hands. I washed them over and over for about two weeks before I finally got back to what I thought was normal.

It seemed so peaceful while we moved up and down the coast of Okinawa. I began to wonder what all the fuss was about. I didn't know about all the big Japanese guns waiting in hidden caves along the beach. They could have taken us out at any time—we were as close as a mile at some points—but they were waiting for *the* invasion and didn't want to reveal their positions.

On Easter Sunday in 1945, our full fleet assembled—troop ships, cruisers, battleships, and all. The troop ships began to send landing boats filled with soldiers and marines to the island; that island lit up and came alive. All the big guns the Japanese had hidden there opened up. Our cruisers and battleships began lobbing big shells over our heads at the island. The ships were about seven or eight miles away and could not be seen over the horizon, but we could hear the shells screaming above us, exploding all over the island. It was a strange feeling, a feeling of power to hear and see the big shells flying over us, pounding a frightening cadence.

All the while our destroyers came within three or four miles of the island, firing their five-inch guns at the exposed Japanese positions in the caves. We were well within the sight and range of the big Japanese guns, but we didn't take any hits.

The fleet of metal and men providing cover fire for the troop ships was successful; the Marines and the Army established their beachhead that same day in a very bloody battle and at a terrible cost. Our ship lucked out and didn't get a scratch . . . that time. But those of us who had been indoctrinated in the art of war got a taste of the real war to come.

After several years of wholesale killing and maiming by the Axis powers, and the wanton destruction of irreplaceable treasures of art and architecture throughout Europe, the Allies finally gained the upper hand. Surrounding the Nazi forces and Berlin, the German capital, to stop the madness, the Allies forced a surrender and ended the bitter struggle over Europe.

By that time the Japanese had gotten so desperate they were using fighter planes as guided missiles. They took young men and trained them in the basics of flying. When ordered, the pilots strapped themselves in a plane and were given a mock funeral; the plane was then loaded with bombs and filled with gasoline. They would fly the planes into our ships in an effort to sink them. It was a suicide mission; the planes and pilots were known as kamikazes. They were taking their toll on our fleet of destroyers. I heard we were losing as many as twenty ships in one day at times.

After a few weeks our ship got orders to proceed to Picket #3, a position between Japan and Okinawa. There were about five destroyers at that station. Our combined job was to shoot down as many of the enemy planes going down to attack the main fleet as we could. It was one of those missions we knew was very dangerous.

The suicide planes would usually strike at sundown, from out of the sun and over the horizon, so they were harder to see and harder to hit with our anti-aircraft weapons. It also made it harder to find and rescue the sailors who had abandoned ship, or those who had been blown overboard, because darkness would soon follow the fight.

By that time I had been through Pearl Harbor and many other engagements, and I had heard of so many of my Navy friends that had been killed, I became callous and indifferent about death. It didn't get to me psychologically at the time.

On one particular evening, May 3, 1945, as the sun was about to go down, the loudspeakers sounded out, "General Quarters! General Quarters!" As the bell rang, I grabbed my life jacket and helmet and ran to my battle station. I was assigned to damage control. My job was to put out fires and rescue the wounded. As soon as I got to my station, I lay on my stomach on the deck. The first plane struck with a terrible explosion, and I felt myself being slammed up against the overhead.

The kamikaze plane had hit the deck directly below the one I was lying on, and the explosion had lifted me in the air. I seemed to slowly float for a split second, and then I came down.

I lay there for a fraction of time. Everything was seen in slow motion; I seemed to comprehend all that was in my field of vision. In front of me I saw what looked like one of my shoes. I thought, The blast has blown my shoes off my feet! My God, my legs are probably gone! I was afraid to look at my legs. I placed my arms at my sides and slowly felt down my body. . . . They were there, thank God. I pushed myself up from the deck; there was a little pain in my shoulder, but at the time it did not matter.

I started to stand and reached out for my shoes; strewn all over the deck in front of me were bundles of money. The money safe's door had been blown open. It was the damnedest thing I had ever seen. For a fraction of a second I wanted to save some of that cash, but my job was to put out fires and try to save lives, so I couldn't do it. I put my shoes on and began to survey the damage.

I stood up and ran through a passageway. As I emerged, I found I was looking directly into the face of the pilot of another kamikaze plane about to hit. My mind seemed aware of every sound, every movement about the deck—it seemed as unreal then as it does now. As the kamikaze hit the ship, the plane, bombs, and gasoline exploded. It blew me into the air a second time, about fifteen feet up off the deck and clear across to the other side of the ship.

It took a while for everything to settle down; I knew we were in big trouble. The large guns were firing, and then I heard the smaller millimeter guns fire rapidly—another plane was about to hit. *Wham!* This one did not propel me into the air, so I pushed myself up again. Directly in front of me was a single one-dollar bill from the safe. I picked it up and put it in my pocket.

The anti-aircraft guns were still hammering away at those planes. I looked around and saw what I thought to be a fire hose. I reached down and picked up what turned out to be a heavy power line that had been severed in the blast. I held on to it for a moment, then threw it down, realizing it could be live.

The gasoline had set everything ablaze, and fire was everywhere.

I found a fire hose and grabbed the nozzle; fortunately, the water was on. I was the only one at the head of that two-inch hose for a minute or two. I thought it was going to lift me off the deck. Then a couple more sailors grabbed on.

After that, everything played over and over again. Gunfire, bombs exploding, gasoline fires creating a choking smell and enormous heat. We all thought it would never end. The Japanese kept pounding us. We were attacked by ten suicide planes in the short span of fifty-one minutes, and six managed to crash into the ship.

Some of the sailors panicked and jumped overboard, sure the ship would sink. With only inches of freeboard between the ship and sure death, some must have thought it would be only seconds before we went down. All four of the other ships with us had been sunk. I saw two go down at the same time with all hands aboard.

It was getting dark, and many of the kids were still jumping overboard—the worst thing they could have done. In the dark they drifted away on currents, never to be seen again. We had had a crew of around three hundred. We lost about forty men in an hour or so. There had been eight of us in my damage control group. God saved only me.

There were some courageous young boys on the big guns who stayed at their stations right up to their deaths. They gave those planes one hell of a fight, looking down the sights of the anti-aircraft guns right into the face of the enemy and only thinking about the job that had to be done.

The *Aaron Ward* had only six black sailors aboard. I was one of those six and was in charge of them all. All those men were assigned to the ammunition magazines. When General Quarters sounded, they went down below deck into the magazines and sent ammunition up to the guns on elevators. The hatches were dogged shut behind them to prevent the ship from sinking too fast if she were hit. It was probably the most dangerous duty aboard our ship, or any ship for that matter. Many a black sailor was lost that way. They couldn't get out in time, even if they had known the ship was sinking, and so they went down to their graves.

If the *Aaron Ward* had gone down we would have lost our black stewards the same way. That's why when every now and then I hear, "You were a cook, you didn't fight," I get very angry. We had the most hazardous jobs of all. When the bell clanged and the command was General Quarters, everybody dropped what they were doing and went to their combat assignment, including the cooks, stewards, and mess attendants. I have nothing but respect for all the black sailors who died so gallantly. Many of those men who went down with the ship survived in total darkness, deep in the ocean, until their oxygen ran out. You never hear about those sailors.

In the case of the *Aaron Ward*, when the Japanese planes got through with us, we were dead in the water. The ship had no power, so we couldn't fire our guns anymore. The mess attendants came out of the magazine and went to the first aid station. No one told them to do it, but as other boys were jumping overboard, Eurice (the officers' cook and only Filipino aboard), Gaines, S. Scott, W. Scott, Wise, and Young—all mess attendants—were there helping the doctor administer to the wounded. They had even taken off their life jackets and helmets.

At that point I was carrying the injured up to first aid to try to save some of them. After we had gathered all the living, we began to pick up the dead. Body parts were embedded in the twisted metal of the planes and of the ship itself. Oil, gasoline, water, and blood made the deck slippery as ice.

We stacked the bodies and body parts on the deck of the ship. When we were through, we had a stack three to four feet high. I knew many of them.

Another destroyer towed us in with a line about three hundred yards long. Even as the destroyer towed us, she was being attacked and was putting up a hell of a fight in the darkness. Because it was pitch black, the Japanese couldn't see us; otherwise they would have finished us off.

After being towed all night, we reached the island of Kara Rette the next morning about sunup. As the destroyer towed us into the harbor, we passed ship after ship that was too damaged to sail. They were in long lines on both sides of us. Some were from a battle the night before—we could tell because they still had stacks of bodies covered with canvas on deck, the same as us. Most would be removed that same day and put in freezers on a ship specifically for that purpose. The ship would take some to be buried at sea, but most were taken for burial to new cemeteries the Army and Navy had opened on Guam and other islands.

The next morning, I sat up on deck. My trousers were caked with dried blood; the smell of death, a smell one never forgets, was everywhere. As I looked at the destruction around me, I realized that all us black sailors had done would be forgotten soon. We would go back to the States, and nothing will have changed for any of us, in the Navy or elsewhere. I hoped it wouldn't be that way, but in 1945, I didn't think we would get any attention. As I got to my feet I realized I had a sharp pain in my shoulder. I went to Dr. Barberi and found out it was broken. He asked me if I wanted to go to the hospital in Guam. I told him no and asked him to patch me up and let me go home on the *Aaron Ward*.

Later Captain Sanders came to me and told me he had heard about the great job we stewards and mess attendants had done the night before. He assured me that when we reached the States he was going to get us some special recognition for a job well done.

We knew we had taken more hits than any destroyer during the war and couldn't be sunk. We had shot down a number of planes also. The men walked around like zombies that next morning. The reality of war had gotten to them. Many of the seventeen- and eighteen-year-old boys now knew what it meant to be a survivor after seeing all those dead and wounded.

I was twenty-eight by then, and all the viciousness and destruction I had witnessed had rendered me indifferent to death. I no longer had the same perspective I once had. It took me several years to come around and recover the compassion that had once been a part of me. My wife Florence prayed for me. I know it helped.

The *Aaron Ward* was to go down in history as the ship that took the most hits during World War II and refused to sink. They made movies, wrote books and magazine articles, and performed reenactments on the radio about us for years afterward.

Kamikaze Attack!*
by
C.B.M. John W. Oden, USN

The story of the *Aaron Ward* is a story of as great gallantry as ever was displayed by the crew of an American naval vessel.

Admiral Chester W. Nimitz gave this high naval accolade:

"Congratulations on your magnificent performance! We all admire a ship that can't be licked!"

A further account by Chief Bosn. Mate John W. Oden:

"The fire on deck was so hot we couldn't get closer than fifty feet at first, but there was desperate need to get it under control. Many air and water lines and much of the communications wiring of the ship passed through the blazing area. Those vital services had to be protected. Also, on a 'can,' any hit is near ammo. Clark, Berkley, and others stayed with the fire."

Account of W. H. Sanders, Jr., Commander, U.S. Navy Commanding Officer

I find it very difficult to express adequately how I feel toward this gallant ship, her officers, and her men. Throughout the period, from the day of commissioning to the present, you have made my job comparatively easy through your fine cooperation, industry, and brave conduct under fire. Our country has always been proud of the

---

* *Battlefield Magazine*, published by Male Publishing Corporation,Office of Publication, 655 Madison Ave., New York, NY (excerpt)

American boys' ability to come through in any emergency, and you, a ship's company, hand-picked by fate, knowing and believing in that for which you were fighting, have by your magnificent fighting spirit confirmed that belief in the minds of your countrymen.

For those of you who will remain in the Naval Service, I say I am happy in the thought that we may again be shipmates. To the "potential civilians" among us, I wish health and happiness, and in your chosen career may you each meet with that full measure of success so characteristic of your short tour on the "Gallant Ward." To the relatives of those boys who gave their lives that we may henceforth live in peace, I say in behalf of all officers and men that we offer you, humbly, our sympathy for the heartaches you have suffered.

May I repeat what I have said elsewhere, "That the ship was saved to fight again, after such punishment in the face of overwhelming odds, bears witness to the wonderful work and the high caliber of fighting officers and men I have had the good fortune of having been assigned my command. I cannot say enough to express my complete admiration of you."

The Captain's Message is taken from the USS *Aaron Ward*'s Documentary Pamphlet, edited by Lieutenant L. Lavrakas, U.S.N., originated by the *Aaron Ward*'s Crew, 1945.

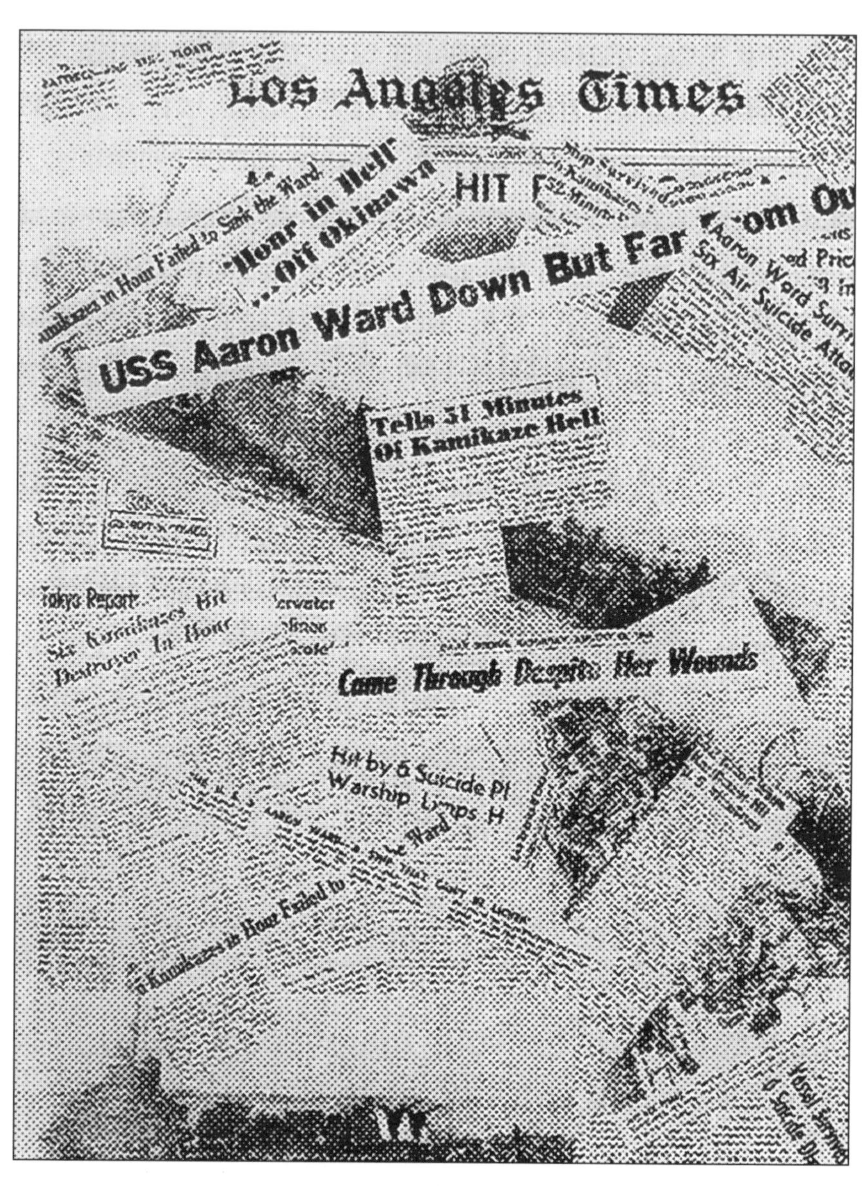

"HEADLINES," from state side

THE SECRETARY OF THE NAVY
WASHINGTON

The President of the United States takes pleasure in presenting the PRESIDENTIAL UNIT CITATION to the

UNITED STATES SHIP AARON WARD

for service as set forth in the following

CITATION:

"For extraordinary heroism in action as a Picket Ship on Radar Picket Station during a coordinated attack by approximately twenty-five Japanese aircraft near Okinawa on May 3, 1945. Shooting down two Kamikazes which approached in determined suicide dives, the U.S.S. AARON WARD was struck by a bomb from a third suicide plane as she fought to destroy this attacker before it crashed into her superstructure and sprayed the entire area with flaming gasoline. Instantly flooded in her after engineroom and fireroom, she battled against flames and exploding ammunition on deck and, maneuvering in a tight circle because of damage to her steering gear, countered another coordinated suicide attack and destroyed three Kamikazes in rapid succession. Still smoking heavily and maneuvering radically, she lost all power when her forward fireroom flooded under a seventh suicide plane which dropped a bomb close aboard and dived in flames into the main deck. Unable to recover from this blow before an eighth bomber crashed into her superstructure bulkhead only a few seconds later, she attempted to shoot down a ninth Kamikaze diving toward her at high speed and, despite the destruction of nearly all her gun mounts aft when this plane struck her, took under fire the tenth bomb-laden plane, which penetrated the dense smoke to crash on board with a devastating explosion. With fires raging uncontrolled, ammunition exploding and all engineering spaces except the forward engineroom flooded as she settled in the water and listed to port, she began a nightlong battle to remain afloat and, with the assistance of a towing vessel, finally reached port the following morning. By her superb fighting spirit and the courage and determination of her entire company, the AARON WARD upheld the finest traditions of the United States Naval Service."

For the President,
James Forrestal
Secretary of the Navy

6974

"PRESIDENTIAL CITATION"

Address not the signer of this Bureau of Naval Personnel, Department, Washington 25, D. C.

Refer to No. Pers-10

NAVY DEPARTMENT
BUREAU OF NAVAL PERSONNEL
WASHINGTON 25, D. C.

Clark

for PEACE ... BUY SAVINGS BONDS

-7 FEB 1947

To: CLARK, Carl Edward, Stl, 371 96 96, USN cab
US Naval Receiving Station
Brooklyn, New York

Via: Commanding Officer.

Subject: Presidential Unit Citation awarded U.S.S. Aaron Ward (DD-483).

1. Forwarded herewith is a facsimile of the Presidential Unit Citation awarded the U.S.S. Aaron Ward.

2. By virtue of your service in the AARON WARD during the period mentioned in the citation, you are hereby authorized to wear as part of your uniform the Presidential Unit Citation ribbon with star, one of which is transmitted herewith.

By direction of Chief of Naval Personnel:

J O Bernier
Assistant to Director,
Medals and Awards.

Encl:
1. Facsimile of citation.
2. Insignia (ribbon bar and star).

- - -

End-1 NSCS, Bayonne, N. J.: 18 Apr 47

From: Supply Officer in Command
To: CLARK, Carl Edward, ST1, 371 96 96, USN

1. Delivered with congratulations.

N H Anderson
N H ANDERSON
By direction 5239

"PRESIDENTIAL UNIT CITATION," Carl E.Clark ST1

Ribbons and medals awarded to Mr.Clark during WW2 aboard the *Aaron Ward*.

pieces 18

Our Return

It took about three weeks for the repair ship at Ulithi to patch up the *Aaron Ward* so we could try to bring her back to the States. We were very anxious and apprehensive due to the fact that we only had half the power and no firepower at all. We had to sail through those dangerous waters unprotected. The gods must have been with us, though, because we were lucky enough not to run into any trouble, even though it took us about two weeks to sail all the way back to the States.

The crew of the *Aaron Ward* had left the States with a core of a few older men like myself and a majority of starry-eyed, ideological young kids. After a short six months, we brought home a load of men who had been through hell. They realized that as they scraped the blood, guts, and flesh of their shipmates off of the bulkheads and decks of the ship.

The ship was tied up at her pier in San Diego; we stewards were in the wardroom. The officers' families had been waiting and came aboard. The officers' wives knew all of us because of the times they had been guests in the wardroom and the mess attendants had served them. I had made special menus many times when I knew they would be aboard for dinner. Captain Sanders's wife had even asked me for my recipes a couple of times. The captain had told them the story about what we stewards had done. The ladies hugged us, kissed us, and thanked us. We were so glad when they showed us they understood what we had done and appreciated it.

One lady was there who had come all the way from Montana to

thank me for saving her son. We had to leave him in the hospital in Guam, but somehow he had gotten word to his mother about how I had pulled him out of an ammunition locker right before it blew up. She said she would always consider me as one of her sons. I wrote to her for a number of years afterward, then lost track of her. Her last name was Hansen.

All the shipyards along the West Coast were full, and so the Navy decided to send the *Aaron Ward* all the way over to the East Coast to be repaired. With only half power it would be a slower, therefore longer journey. Captain Sanders allowed me to go ahead overland and meet the ship in Brooklyn, New York. I first went to Oakland, where Flo was. While I was gone, she had written me about every other day, but sometimes, because of the war, I would not receive her letters for two or more weeks. It was such a wonderful thing when the mail did catch up with us and I had all those beautiful, warm letters to read. In one letter she described a dream she had had that was almost identical to what had happened to me in Okinawa. She wrote that she was worried and wondered if I was okay. Later, about a week before I returned home, a sailor from another ship told Flo he heard I had been killed. So when I returned home, Flo wasn't expecting me but was waiting instead for a telegram from the president.

After that long period of separation, and having had so little time together before I left, we had a lot of catching up to do. Although you can never really make up time lost, you can always give it an effort. You better believe we made one heck of an effort there in Oakland while waiting to depart for the East Coast. With the war still going on in the Pacific, the trains were crowded with military personnel shuttling between coasts, and the civilian population was in transit as well. Still, we managed to get a berth on the train, though it was designed to sleep only one person. We didn't mind that at all. We were still making up for lost time.

When we got to New York, I reported to the Navy Receiving Ship in Brooklyn. The facilities were buildings used as receiving stations that sailors and marines are assigned to when in transition between duty stations. The Navy had stopped using actual ships quite some time before I joined, but the term "Receiving Ship" was still being used.

Living quarters were very scarce. The YMCA had a referral service to assist people in finding a place to stay, so Flo and I went there to see if we could find a room for rent. We were referred to a couple in Brooklyn with the last name of Clark, the same as ours, so we figured they couldn't be all that bad. We met with them and agreed to pay seven dollars per week for a room, with a community bathroom that we shared with the tenants of two other rental rooms.

Within a week of my reporting to the Receiving Ship, the *Aaron Ward* arrived in New York. The *Ward* was at the Brooklyn Navy Yard, where plans had been made to cut her in half, join the salvageable half with that of another ship, and put her back in action. Captain Sanders took it upon himself to intervene on my behalf and got me assigned to duty on land so that I would not have to go back to sea so soon after our ordeal. It was his way of expressing his appreciation for the effort that I, as well as those stewards under me, had put forth during and after the attack.

I was assigned to a naval facility known as the Lido Beach Hotel at Lido Beach on Long Island. It was a hotel the Navy had taken over to use as a receiving station for the movement of sailors and marines to and from the European Theater. Since the war in Europe had just ended a couple of months earlier, the facility was being used as a discharge station, and there were hundreds of men passing through the facility to be discharged from active duty.

I was assigned as the master-at-arms. A majority of my time was spent rounding up sailors and requesting they return to their assigned stations. Because the guys were still on a military payroll, everybody was assigned a job. And because it was more of a formality, many of the assigned tasks were non-urgent, so some of the men would just go and do something else. Whenever I saw the same man or group of men just sort of hanging out for more than a couple of hours, I figured they were supposed to be somewhere else, and most of the time I was right. So I would instruct them to return to their duty station and then later I would verify that they had found their way to their station.

When I approached one young fellow and asked him where he had been assigned to work, he responded, "Hey, man, the war's over, and I don't think I'm supposed to work anymore." It took me some time to convince him that as long as he wore his uniform and was getting paid, he had to work. None of those guys were punished; they were only sent back to work. I held the position for about four months, and then I was assigned to be a baker. I remained a baker for the remainder of my duty at Lido Beach.

At that particular time, when an individual was discharged, in addition to their separation papers they were also issued a small pin to wear on the lapel of their civilian clothes to show they had served in the armed forces during World War II. The pin was affectionately nicknamed The Ruptured Duck, and most of the guys threw them away because they were so ugly. They were supposed to represent an eagle, but the resemblance was much closer to the nickname given it.

A couple of months after arriving in New York and settling into my routine, the war with Japan ended. In August of 1945 the Japanese surrendered to the Allied forces, and the terrible time of death and destruction ended.

The war in Europe had ended a few months earlier, so now there was peace on all fronts. The desperate demand for more ships ended abruptly, and the *Aaron Ward,* which we had brought all the way back from the South Pacific, would not be repaired. It was sold at some point thereafter to the Gillette Razor Company as scrap metal. I'm sure some of us have probably shaved with part of her.

Flo and I had arrived in New York at the beginning of summer. Fall came and went, and winter was soon upon us. It gets cold in New York in the winter. When we moved in to our place in Brooklyn, we had not paid close attention to the fact that the heat was not working. It would get so cold in our room that my beer would freeze. When I got up to go to work, Flo would get up and have some coffee and a roll, then get dressed and bundled up as if she were going out in order to sit in our room. It didn't take long to figure out we had to find another place. Flo had managed to meet and make friends with some nice folks, so we had places where we could spend some time in warmth. We were there a total of four months before we moved.

We decided that Flo should try to get a live-in position out on Long Island. She was successful in getting a position in a well-to-do area right in Lido Beach. Florence was to work for a Mrs. Edwards, the widow of the former mayor of Lido Beach. She had been widowed just three months before we moved in. Her husband had been killed, shot down by his own security guard. We had been reading about it in the papers before we moved in, not even imagining we would wind up involved with the family.

Florence's job was to cook and serve the meals for Mrs. Edwards, her daughter, and any other invited guests. We had our own separate, self-contained apartment (maid's quarters). And to top it off, it was only a couple of miles from my job. While we were living in Brooklyn, I had spent over an hour each way traveling to and from work. Now life was good once again.

Every time Mrs. Edwards had guests for a meal, she would ask me to come into the drawing room in my uniform so she could show me off to her guests. After Flo had finished cooking and serving the meal, Mrs. Edwards would ask her if she would honor them with a few selections on the giant grand piano in the drawing room. Flo was a graduate in music from Xavier University in New Orleans. She could play Beethoven, Brahms, Mozart, or any other classics, as well as anything contemporary. Mrs. Edwards always paid her extra when she played.

Everything was going fine until one day Flo told me that Mrs. Edwards's man friend had approached her in an unacceptable manner. We moved out the next day.

After leaving Mrs. Edwards, Flo and I moved to Rockville Center on Long Island. We rented a room from an elderly couple by the name of Brown. It was about five miles from Lido Beach, but it was still closer than when we lived in Brooklyn.

Shortly after we moved, the Lido Beach Hotel closed down. I had been there about a year. During that year, hundreds and hundreds of men came through, mustering out of the Navy, and then the massive flow became a trickle.

With the closing of the Lido Beach Hotel, I went back to the Receiving Ship in Brooklyn. I was there about three weeks before being assigned to the Naval Officers Supply School in Bayonne, New Jersey, as a butcher. I was responsible for cutting all the meat to feed a couple hundred student officers and the administration and faculty of about twenty-five officers. I also held classes to teach the student officers butchering.

One Saturday morning during formation there was to be a ceremony in which I would formally be awarded my Purple Heart for the broken shoulder I received on the *Aaron Ward*. The young officers were mumbling about their discontent with having to attend a ceremony in which a black sailor was receiving a medal. The commanding officer stopped it by saying, "This Saturday's shore leave might possibly be delayed." With that, the formation came to attention and the ceremony was concluded without a hitch. Here I was a ten-year veteran of the Navy being awarded a Purple Heart for being wounded in combat, and because I was a black steward, the commanding officer had to threaten the white officers with delayed shore leave in order for me to get the respect I was entitled to.

Purple Heart for injuries received while serving aboard the *Aaron Ward*, May 3, 1945

Mr. Clark receiving Purple Heart, May 3, 1945

pieces 19

The Mighty Mouse

Now that World War II was over, our Navy had many surplus ships. They decided to give some of the ships to our allied countries, and the small ones like the mine sweepers, submarine chasers, and PT boats were given to different domestic entities such as the Navy Reserve, Sea Scouts, and other such organizations.

I had just received orders to report to the Naval Receiving Ship in Brooklyn to see what the Navy had in store for me next. When I arrived, I couldn't believe how many of the previously discharged men were there trying to reenlist after finding that civilian life had gotten too rough. Even more interesting was the fact that most of the men had been given the option to stay in the Navy when they were discharged and had made the decision to leave. Some would probably change their minds too late, as they had to exercise the option to stay within three months. Then there were those who had been exposed to civilian life for as little as a month or so and had returned unshaven, unwashed, and broke to reenlist.

I had been in New York for about two months now waiting for my orders. In the meantime, I was cooking breakfast and lunch for the captain of the Receiving Ship. The captain had his evening meal at home, and I liked that because I could go home after the lunch meal to be with Flo. I got a seven dollar a week room and spent a lot of time at Ebbits Field watching the Brooklyn Dodgers play.

One beautiful morning in May, after returning from liberty, I was told to come down to the assembly room at the Receiving Ship.

When I got the word to report, I became apprehensive; I knew it could be some bad news. I was thinking that I probably would be sent somewhere I didn't like. When I got there, ten other sailors were already in the assembly room.

An officer entered the room and greeted us; he then informed us that we had all been selected for a special project. We were then given the details of the assignment. The Navy had given a submarine chaser to the city of Cincinnati, Ohio, and we were to deliver the ship to Cincinnati. The officer giving us the instructions was smiling at times and seemed to be treating the entire affair as if it were a joke.

There was a chart on the wall showing the proposed route, which made it look serious enough, but I said to myself, "Could this assignment be all that it is cracked up to be or is there a hidden agenda?" We all looked at each other, and some of the sailors began making small jokes about the assignment. There were three young kids in the group; all the rest of us were old salts, and we were making the jokes because we knew about those little ships.

The ship was to be used to train sailors in the Naval Reserve in Cincinnati. Most of us old salts had seen the little ships at one time or another, and we all considered them nothing but a joke. They were made of wood, about a hundred feet long, and somewhat fast in the water. Their job originally was to chase down submarines and then drop depth charges on them.

I looked around at all the other sailors who had been assigned with me; most were older sailors like myself who had just come off one of the big war ships. Chief Petty Officer Cannon was the most impressive of our group of sailors. He had been the skipper of one of the war ships that patrolled the waters off Alaska during the war. He was a big burly man with a red beard and a booming voice to go with it. I was a steward first class at the time and had been in the Navy for about nine years.

The Navy officer said, "As you all know, the only way to get this ship from Brooklyn to Cincinnati is to take her down the East Coast to Florida, then through the Gulf of Mexico to New Orleans, then on up the Mississippi River to the Ohio River to Cincinnati. You have two months to do this. Chief Cannon, you will have most of the responsibility for this ship. Clark, you will have charge of the Navy

The mighty *Mighty Mouse*, a wooden submarine chaser.

vouchers to buy all the food and supplies." There were two other sailors who knew how to operate and maintain the diesel motors and a chief in charge of keeping the ship clean and shipshape. Chief Cannon made contact with the paymaster in Brooklyn—pay that was due would be wired to ports along the way.

The next day we moved aboard the ship in a military manner. I was the only black in the crew; I went aboard and looked at the galley and the facilities and then made my list of supplies needed. We were issued one Navy .45-caliber pistol, the only firepower we had. We then went over to the supply depot to get the first load of supplies. When we returned to the ship we unloaded our supplies on the pier and instructed a young sailor to stay with them and keep the

.45 with him. We knew as hard as times were in Brooklyn—and every place else for that matter—somebody just might cart them off. By the time we got back to the dock with our last load of supplies, the young sailor, who was from Brooklyn, was stretched out upon the supplies, fast asleep. When we woke the dummy up he started reaching for the .45—it was not there. Someone had stolen the gun. That was the last thing we expected to happen. It was probably an omen of all the crazy things that were to follow. Lucky for us the thief hadn't taken any supplies, but maybe they should have taken the guard.

After about three or four days of preparing for the journey we were ready to shove off. Then the Navy for some reason decided to send a young officer aboard as our captain. He was fresh out of the Naval Academy. We could see he was awestruck as he came aboard to find all of us old war veterans as his crew. He was almost young enough to be an old salt's son.

Us old salts had done all there was to do to get underway, and Chief Cannon was definitely the man in charge. I guess the young officer thought the ship was in good hands, because he stayed out of our way. One of the more imaginative sailors decided that the ship needed a name and suggested we call it *Mighty Mouse.* The name stuck. To us veterans it was more of a joke than a ship.

Finally we got underway. We were to only travel during daytime and pull in to port each evening. The first port we pulled in to was in Virginia; it was there the fabric began to unravel. Someone mentioned we needed some beer. I heard, "How about it, Clark, you got the vouchers?"

All of us knew it was a cardinal sin to have alcohol aboard a Navy vessel, but we all seemed to say at the same time, "Ah, what the hell, we deserve it!"

Two other sailors and I went ashore to buy about five cases of beer with the vouchers. The three of us walked into the store, picked up the five cases of beer, and stacked them by the door. I walked up to the counter with the vouchers and told the clerk, "Just put it down as canned goods."

The clerk asked, "By God, can I do that?"

"Hell yeah!"

While I handled the paperwork, the rest of the guys began cart-ing the beer back to the ship. When I got back to the ship I made room in the refrigerator so when we wanted a cold one, it would be right there. The young officer with his one little stripe just stood there.

With everybody happy now, we shoved off again. We pulled into a little place in North Carolina the next day. The sailors took liberty in the little town; the country girls just loved them. They were having such a good time we stayed for three days. One of the sailors found a little Scotty dog and brought it aboard. Now we had a mascot, appropriately named "Scotty."

When we left there we were three days behind schedule; now we had to try and make it up, so we pushed the *Mighty Mouse* to her limits and wound up burning out one of our engines. We were then directed by the Navy to take the *Mighty Mouse* to the Navy Shipyard in Charleston, South Carolina, to wait for a new engine, which would be sent down in about thirty days.

The first evening after we arrived at the Ship Yard, one of the younger kids from aboard ship went ashore and stole a motor scooter from the base. Before he could return the scooter and get back aboard ship, he crashed the scooter into the Ship Yard captain's wife's car. We never heard from him again.

It was getting close to Christmastime. By then we had gotten so far away from Navy regulations we were on our own, for sure. With the engine down, some of the more imaginative sailors suggested that rather than all of us wait there for the ship to be repaired, we all just go home and either come back when the ship was ready or, for the fellows who lived along the route, meet the ship at a port nearby. All of the crew again seemed to say at the same time, "That's a damned good idea!"

We decided that we should leave a way for the young officer to get in contact with us when the ship was ready. So on a piece of paper we all wrote down our names, addresses, and phone numbers to give to the officer in charge. Chief Cannon volunteered to give the captain the list. What we didn't know then was that the chief did not hand the list to the captain. The captain was away—probably at the Officers' Club having a martini.

We didn't learn until we returned to the *Mighty Mouse* that the list had been pinned to the captain's door. None of us had been authorized to leave—we just left.

Sometime after we had left, the captain of the base came down to the dock to see about the *Mighty Mouse* and its crew. The only person aboard was the young officer.

"Where the hell is the crew?" the captain asked him.

"They all went home."

Then the captain yelled, "Bring all of their asses back here—and you're fired!"

None of it sat well with the captain, especially since one of our crew had stolen a motor scooter the first night we were there and ran into his wife's car.

A short time after the base captain fired the young officer, the *Mighty Mouse* got her new engine and a new skipper, Chief Cannon. Most of the crew was aboard now and ready to go on down the coast to Florida. All we needed to do was pick up the remaining crewmembers along the route.

We finally got back out to sea. I was hoping that all the bad luck was behind us, but I was wrong. One day, while I was cooking in the galley, I had a large pan of hot oil on the stove to fry some french fries. Here comes this dumb young sailor who wanted some ice cubes for a drink. He banged the ice tray on the counter and one of the ice cubes bounced into the hot oil. The oil splashed out of the pan and onto the stove and caught my galley on fire. It took two or three of us with fire extinguishers to get the fire under control, which took some time. I was thinking, What can happen next? I began to wonder if this was the way the rest of our journey would be. I was soon to find out.

We pulled into Miami, Florida, on a beautiful sunny afternoon and tied up at the Coast Guard base. Chief Cannon had told us about his rich aunt who lived there. He told everybody on board his aunt knew we were coming and had planned a party for us aboard the *Mighty Mouse*, breaking regulations again.

It was no joke; his aunt had her chauffeur drive out to the pier where we were tied up in this long limousine. The driver began to unload about two cases of whiskey and two or three cases of beer. She had even catered food, complete with balloons and streamers. Chief Cannon told the chauffeur to tell his aunt, "The balloons and streamers are a bit too much and have to go; it does not look Navy."

Then, when the limousine came back about sundown, it was not loaded with balloons but with about nine or ten girls. Some of their heads were sticking up through the sunroof; they were giggling and laughing, ready to party. There were no black ones, so I decided to be cool, but the party was on.

The music was loud, and the more everybody drank the louder the party got. At around nine o'clock the Coast Guard sent some military police down to tell Chief Cannon, "Get this ship the hell off our damn base!" We moved the ship and tied her to a civilian pier a little further down. The girls got louder and the sailors got louder as they each chased and were chased all over that little ship.

I had never seen such activities in my life—everyone was *lettin' loose.* It was getting late, and I was real tired of all the chasing and giggling, so I climbed up in my bunk. It wasn't long before most of the crew—for obvious reasons—ended up in the sleeping area. Chief Cannon and several of the mates were whooping it up and joking about something.

I wasn't paying much attention to what anybody was saying in particular, then I heard Cannon say something about some "nigger" he use to know. It could even have been a nigger joke, I don't know. Like I said, I wasn't paying that much attention then to anything, but when I heard the word nigger, I raised up in my bunk and looked into Chief Cannon's eyes.

"Oh my God, Clark," Cannon said. "I am so sorry. Please don't be upset. I don't know why I said that, but I apologize, please. It wasn't about you!"

I just brushed him off. "Let's talk about it tomorrow," I said.

Suddenly, Chief Cannon decided to cast off and go to sea with all the drunken women still aboard. I begged him not to do it, but to no avail. I thought to myself, "He's probably upset about what he said." I knew that small-craft warnings were out, and the conditions for going to sea in our vessel were unthinkable. The water was much too rough for the little ship, and the fact that everybody was drunk made it even worse. Since I could not talk him out of it I climbed up onto the flying bridge, above all of the drunken sailors and drunken women. They were all arguing over who was going to steer the ship. I called down to them, trying to give instructions to help at least keep the boat in the channel—between the buoys.

I saw the lights of a boat coming into the harbor about a thousand yards away. I called down to those fools below, "Green light, thousand yards!" No one was listening. The lights were closing in on us. First I looked at them and they were green, and a few seconds later they were red, so I knew we were zigzagging across her course. "Green! Red! Green! Red!" I shouted. I looked down at the calamity before me; the drunken women and sailors were still fighting over the wheel. I saw the red light directly ahead and knew we were going to collide. "God help us," I prayed.

We hit a large yacht amidships with a loud crash and knocked a huge hole in her side. I tried to get Cannon to stop, but all he said was, "That will teach you not to cross my bow!" Thank God no one was hurt on our ship; we didn't know about the yacht's crew. We learned later that the yacht did sink.

Our little ship was all over the place. I had been through the war, had seen many battles, and I thought, Wouldn't it be a shame to die because of these fools? After we got to sea the conditions were just as bad as I had feared; we were barely able to keep the ship from capsizing. The girls were beginning to sober up by now, and most of them were seasick as hell.

One of the girls came to me and said, "I'm scared to death. Do you know how to pray?"

"Of course I know how to pray."

"How do you do it?"

I could see she was desperate; she was only about eighteen or nineteen years old.

I told her, "Just talk to God and tell him how scared you are; maybe you will feel better."

In the meantime, most of the girls were mad as hell and letting all of us know it by the names they were calling us. For sure the crewmen had realized by now what a mistake they had made and were seriously trying to save their butts. The seriousness of the moment included navigating in the keys, trying to avoid the rocks.

The next morning we reached Key West, Florida. Only God knows how we missed all of those rocks. The girls were all hung over and still raising hell, asking, "How are we going to get back to Miami?" Cannon asked all of us if we had enough money to buy the women tickets for a bus back to Miami—we did. We gave the more responsible looking one the money for the tickets, and off they went.

We had no schedule now; it was almost as if the Navy had forgotten about us. So we decided to stay a week in Key West and fish. The fishing was excellent. After a week we left, our next stop being Mobile, Alabama. Our ship was in need of supplies, so we stopped and docked at a pier. A couple of sailors and I went over to this very small store for the supplies. I was in my uniform, and these people were referring to me as the "government man." Among other things I bought were five smoked hams. I decided to send one of them to Flo in New York. Meat was still being rationed; I knew all my friends would be so glad to get part of that twenty-pound ham.

Cannon and another sailor found two guys who claimed to be down on their luck and needed a ride to Memphis, Tennessee. Cannon brought them back to the ship and turned them over to me and told me I could use them to wash dishes and help me in the galley. There wasn't much to do, but I took them in. They seemed to be nice guys but very talkative, and they drank a lot of our beer.

So we were off to our next stop—Biloxi, Mississippi. We reached Biloxi soon after nightfall. The weather was bad and we had to find somewhere to tie the *Mouse* up. When we approached the pier, the Stars and Stripes were flying on the *Mouse*. There was a little shack visible in the dock area. Chief Cannon, beard and all, was up on the flying bridge. He asked permission to tie up; the guy who was sitting in the little shack didn't answer him. So as they eased the ship up to the dock, I hopped off and took a turn around the cleat with the bowline, and that little old crooked man ran out with an ax and chopped the line off.

I took another turn, and he did it again. Then he stood in front of me with the ax poised and said, "I can chop them off faster than you can put them on, boy."

I told Cannon, "Forget it," as I hopped back aboard.

We then just let the *Mouse* drift for a while and drifted into some trees. We tied the *Mighty Mouse* right there to a tree; it seemed so unladylike to me. We stayed there overnight and left at first light for New Orleans. I was anxious to get there because Flo had gone to college there and had given me the addresses of some of her lady friends. The other sailors had heard about New Orleans and were anxious to get there as well.

We arrived the next evening. I put on a clean uniform and went to town. I stopped to get a haircut and then I was off to visit my wife's friends. They showed me a wonderful time.

While there one evening, I decided to go down to Rampart Street. The sailors had told me that was where the action was, but Flo's friends had also said I should be careful. I stopped in a bar, ordered a drink, and promptly got robbed. The proprietor had conveniently gone to the storeroom. I thought, Hard head! Flo's friends told me to stay away from here—good enough for me.

We stayed in New Orleans for three weeks. We were there so long because we were all having such a good time. A couple of the sailors fell in love and didn't want to leave at all, but we had to get underway.

It was now time to go on up the Mississippi. We had to have a river pilot because the river was tricky and changed a lot. There were sandbars along the river that constantly moved; only the river pilot knew how to navigate them safely. Our pilot was a native Southerner; he soon let me know that for sure by the comment he made the first day he was aboard. After sizing me up he said, "Boy, you sho gonna like it down heah in that uniform—all the colored gals gonna be afta you."

I told him, "Don't talk to me; just leave me alone." He did, but now and then I would see him looking at me, trying to figure me out.

About the second day, as we sailed up the river, three of us were sitting on the deck talking when all of a sudden we heard a *ping!* As we all looked around, trying to figure out what was going on, there was another *ping!* One of the sailors felt a sting on his back. He placed his hand where he had felt the pain; when he removed his hand, there was blood on it. Some fool was shooting at us from the riverbank.

We all went inside. The sailor only had a crease where the bullet had just broken the skin. The riverbanks at that point were about half a mile away. We kept a sharp eye out but did not see anything and thought it would not happen again. We continued on up the river.

I think I saw just about every foot of the Mississippi River. I

Here I am going up the Mississippi River on *Mighty Mouse*; heading for Cincinnati, Ohio, 1946.

would sit up on deck and just watch the scenery go by. It was really something to see—the big white mansions high on the hills, gleaming in the sunlight, and then right down by the river the weather-beaten shacks where the poor black folks and poor whites lived.

The riverboats came and went. Some still had a big paddle wheel on the stern. Most were diesel powered and pushed large barges with cars, grain, and almost anything else imaginable up and down the river. Most were going to New Orleans to have their cargo loaded on ships.

The bums we had picked up were still with us, and things were fairly normal now. Everybody seemed happy, with good food and plenty of beer. The river pilot took me at my word and didn't say anything else to me.

We arrived in Rosedale, Arkansas, where we picked up the sailor who had left Charleston, South Carolina, ahead of us. He had told his mother we were coming for him; she lived around there somewhere. The sailor and his mother came down along the riverbanks and met the *Mouse*. He asked her to come aboard and bake an apple cobbler for the crew.

She did and it was terrible—the worst cobbler I had ever tasted. I felt good about her failure because that sailor was the only one I didn't like. I had had a run-in with him; he told me one day about how good he felt the colored folks down in Arkansas were and how well they knew how to stay in their place, and he said they really knew how to treat white folks—I knocked the hell out of him. A few days later he apologized, but I knew I had to watch him from then on.

We left Rosedale in the morning and traveled until about one or two o'clock before someone mentioned that we hadn't seen Scotty, our mascot, all day. We searched the ship, and Scotty was not aboard. We knew then that when we had let him off that morning he hadn't gotten back on. We turned the ship around and went all the way back to where we had been tied up along the riverbank. As we got within a quarter mile or so, we could see Scotty jumping up and down—he was so glad to see that boat. He had waited all day for us to come back for him.

Now that we were all together again we headed off to Memphis, Tennessee. I, as usual, sat up on deck watching the scenery go by. The giant whirlpools in the river fascinated me. My job was easy and even enjoyable with those two guys aboard to clean up my kitchen and peel potatoes and such. I knew I would soon lose them; they would leave when we reached Memphis that evening. We arrived in Memphis about sundown, and I said good-bye to both of the men. By then I was anxious to get the trip over with and get back to my wife in New York. We were in Memphis for two days, I had not left the ship, and I felt it was time to get going on up the river.

It was the fall season. We were going north, and the nights were beginning to get rather chilly. The *Mouse* didn't have any heat. I hung a fan in the doorway of the galley to blow the heat from the galley into the living quarters; it kept us fairly warm.

Our next stop would be Cairo, Illinois, where the Mississippi and the Ohio Rivers met. We were to stay there overnight and then head on to Cincinnati. When we reached Cairo we tied the *Mouse* up at a pier across from a diesel boat that pushed barges up and down the river.

That one was on its way up the Mississippi to collect some

Scotty, the *Mighty Mouse* mascot

barges and move them back down the river. I saw a black woman on the barge deck. I went down on our deck and we began to talk. She asked me if I wanted to come over that evening and visit. I did go over when I got through feeding my crew.

Ruby was quite a person, I soon found out. I was in my early thirties; Ruby was about sixty-five or so. She told me she had been riding the riverboats since she was nineteen years old. She served me some black-eyed peas and cornbread. We also had a bottle of Jack Daniel's. Ruby said she didn't have a man now but she told me about some of the husbands she had had—it seemed there were quite a few. One in particular she described as a "fast-talking dandy" from New Orleans. She said he later ran away with a "high yeller" in Memphis, Tennessee. "Lord, how that man could talk and play that piano," she said. I think he was the one she loved the most.

We talked until late in the night. She told me about floods, boat collisions, catfish she had caught, and some she had only seen. She said one was so big she thought it was a log. She told me about some of the cabarets and joints she used to go to in New Orleans and the other cities along the river. I finally left about one o'clock feeling really good that I had met Ruby.

We left early the next morning; we wanted to reach Cincinnati before dark. The weather was cold now; the Ohio River was beginning to freeze over. We arrived at about four or five in the evening. The press was there to greet us, along with a small welcoming party. They wrote us up and mentioned us on the radio. We were anxious to get back to Brooklyn, though. We left that night on the train, Scotty and all, and arrived in Brooklyn the next day—four months after we had begun the fated trip, which was scheduled to take sixty days.

The next morning I was told to report to the assembly room at nine o'clock. When I got there, all the rest of the *Mighty Mouse* crew was also there. We were all anxious to know what it was all about; we all suspected we might be in big trouble because we had done so many things wrong on the cruise. We were told to board a Navy bus and that we were going over to Manhattan, to the Navy Headquarters.

When we reached the headquarters we were ushered into a hallway and told to have a seat on these long, shiny wooden benches. Finally, after a while a lady came out and called, "Carl Clark." I was thinking, What the hell! I'm the only black here and the first to be called when there is trouble. Here I go. Hope I can handle this one—it's got to be bad.

I entered the room and a short, bald-headed man said, "Please, have a seat. I am Commander Kelley with Naval Intelligence, and this is Miss James." He pointed to a woman who sat there with one of those little tape recorders. "Now, is Carl Clark your name, and is this your serial number?"

"Yes."

He said to me, "I will be asking you some questions, and I want your honest answers. . . . Did you and the rest of the crew have beer aboard the ship?"

"Not to my knowledge."

"Did you have unauthorized women aboard?"

"Not to my knowledge."

"Did this ship collide with another ship in Florida?"

"I don't think so."

"Did you have unauthorized passengers aboard?"

"Not to my knowledge."

At that time Commander Kelly told Miss James to stop recording.

He turned to me and said, "We are going to wipe that testimony off . . . . I hope your memory will improve as I ask you these questions again. Now, let's start over."

These people know everything we did, and it doesn't make sense to keep lying, I thought, so I answered the questions correctly the second time.

Commander Kelly then questioned the rest of the crew. I will always remember Cannon pacing up and down in the hallway with that great red beard; he brought to mind Captain Ahab before he went out to face Moby Dick.

After the questioning was over they sent all of us back to Brooklyn. We learned later that the two bums we had picked up in Mobile who had worked for me in the galley and drank all that beer were Naval Intelligence Officers. The Navy had to pay for the yacht in Miami, but they didn't punish any of us. They didn't even put it in our records. I guess, being so soon after the war, they thought we had gone through enough . . . at least that's how I saw it.

pieces 20

Norfolk

Finally my time came to leave New York. My orders said I was to report to the USS *Shenandoah* in Boston, Massachusetts. The ship was in the Navy Shipyard for repairs. After the repairs were made we headed back to Norfolk, Virginia, our home port.

That to me was the same as going back to hell. I knew I would have to face all the raw race hate and segregation, reminding me each day that I had to "stay in my place." Being in uniform didn't mean a thing.

The first thing that happened to remind me of the intimidation and segregation occurred as soon as the ship tied up at the pier. A truck drove up with two water fountains to place on the dock in front of our ship. One was a nice, refrigerated water cooler that was put in place with a sign attached: "White only."

Then they placed a plain old rusty fountain, no refrigeration, with the sign: "Colored only, military included!" I had almost gotten my butt shot off in the war, which had officially ended just a little over three years before. I couldn't get used to that stuff, and I felt anger throughout my body. It was to last the entire five years I was in Norfolk.

I would walk down Church Street and see all the hopelessness, filth, and crime. I felt sorry for the people that society had done this to; so many people. All of the police force was white, and the only time I saw them on Church Street was when a couple of police cars came on Saturday to intimidate some of the black people and beat a few black folks' heads.

Every Saturday and Sunday they picked up a couple of our black sailors. I would have to go down to the police court on Monday mornings after my ship gave me a couple hundred dollars so I could bail them out.

It would always be for something like urinating behind a billboard, or procuring a prostitute, or drinking in public. If I weren't there to bail them out on Monday morning, they would be put on a bus and taken to what was called the "Pea Farm." It was a farm run by civilians. Once the guys were there they had to stay thirty days, working the fields with no pay—a form of modern slavery and political trickery.

It is unfortunate that of all the negative things that have happened to my family and myself in our lives, the most vivid in my memory is Norfolk, Virginia.

There were some pleasant times as well as bad times there, but the good times always seemed to be overshadowed by the bad. The worst thing, I guess, is that the good times had to be dredged out of and through all the muck and mire of racial prejudice and bigotry.

We were fortunate to be involved with and accepted by a group of people who respected and befriended us. Our first lodgings were at Dr. Carnick's house, where we rented the ground floor. They insisted we meet all their friends. We were all young then, and there was a lot of partying going on. Flo loved parties and was an accomplished musician. I had a pretty good voice to boot, so we made a good duo at all the parties. Almost all who came would contribute in some way to the entertainment, so we were in good stead.

Even though Dr. and Mrs. Carnick made our stay in their home comfortable, we knew we had to get a place of our own soon. After about a year my son Karl was born, so we decided to move into an old house across the bay in Berkley, Virginia. I really liked that old house; it was close to an old abandon wooden pier.

Sometimes at night I would go there and catch crabs or just mess around in the water. The best times were when we all would go and just sit down and watch the ships and boats on the water. Now that I look back, I realize that old pier was my most hallowed place. I washed a great deal of bigotry and hatred out of my system at that old pier.

One evening, shortly after I got home from the *Shenandoah*, I was relaxing in my living room and watching my son Karl play out in the front yard. It was a pleasant day; I was still in my uniform, just settling in. Something caught my eye. I looked down the old dusty road that ran in front of our house and noticed this white police officer approaching. I wondered why he was walking casually down our road; I had never seen a policeman on that road before.

When he came adjacent to our house, he approached our yard. Karl, a little over two years old, toddled up to him. "Hi!" said my son. The policeman looked over at him, walked closer, then took out his billy club and bent over my son. He began to grimace and make gestures with his stick as if he were going to hit him. Karl held himself and began to scream. He looked toward the house, terror in his eyes.

I ran out the door and grabbed the cop, adrenaline flowing through my veins; I lifted him up in the air and shook him. His keys and handcuffs were rattling, and his gun was all loose in his holster. Suddenly I realized that my son was there watching me, and that the cop could pull his gun and kill me and no one would do anything to the bastard. I lowered the cop slowly.

We looked at each other eye to eye, and I could see what was on his mind: "I am going to kill this nigger." I turned away, a cold feeling at my back; he had started unbuttoning the holster of his thirty-eight. I swept Karl up and headed for the front door. Maybe because of my uniform, or because I had really shaken him up, or maybe because it just wasn't my time, but he didn't shoot me. He reminded me of one of those white animal hunters; he just plain looked like he was on a hunt down my dusty old street, looking for a nigger to shoot.

I looked out my window at him; he was just standing there with the gun in his hand at his side. He stood there for what seemed like forever, then turned and walked away.

That was the last straw for me. I knew it would be impossible for me to live comfortably in my own home anymore. I had to try and get away from there.

pieces 21

USS Shenandoah

The USS *Shenandoah* was a destroyer tender. Its duty was to provide service and supplies. Our ship was a floating store and more. We had a complete machine shop, movie exchange, camera shop—all you could think of, including a dry cleaners. We did not maneuver with the fleet; we were on a six-month rotation in the Mediterranean Sea with two other tenders.

While the destroyers we supported were on maneuvers, we leisurely moved to where they would come to port next for service, stopping at places all along the way. I guess I've been to every country bordering the Mediterranean Sea—France, Italy, Greece, Portugal, Turkey, and all the North African countries. We spent a lot of time in Naples, Italy. I got to know so many families there, I always looked forward to going.

There was one thing in particular I started while there that I am very proud of. During World War II, the Army had passed through, and the soldiers of one of the black outfits had left a lot of black babies. Most had been given to the orphanages because the populace had declared the little black babies unacceptable, and their mothers as well. One particular young lady was about twenty and had decided to keep her baby. Her family had thrown her out into the streets. She was sleeping in alleys, begging for herself and the baby. She had enough pride not to prostitute herself, so I asked the black guys on the ship to adopt her and the baby. I guess I did a pretty good sell. I wrote up the rules and we decided to take up a collection of two dollars each month from each black sailor to get her a place to stay and so she could support herself and the baby.

There were only about twenty of us black sailors aboard, but we knew she could do very well on forty dollars per month. The first money we gave her was just before Easter. She got all straightened up and asked some of us to go to church with her Easter Sunday. About three other guys and I went with her. She was the star that morning. The priest acknowledged her and asked her to stand up. We all felt great.

I knew that she needed help for longer than we would be in port. Since I was on the ship's welfare committee, I arranged with the other two rotating tenders to carry on the adoption no matter what, and they did.

About twenty years later, I saw an article about those kids in a popular magazine, and in it there was a picture of this beautiful lady and her son, who was standing there with a briefcase in his hand and who was a lawyer in Naples. It was the lady and her son who we had adopted over twenty years earlier. I felt great again.

The prejudice, however, followed us even aboard the *Shenandoah*. One Christmas the ship decided to have the kids from one of the orphanages aboard for a party. Our ship was anchored out in the Naples harbor, so boats had to bring the kids to the ship; when they arrived, about a dozen white sailors were assigned to carry the kids, who were about four or five years old, up the ladder and deposit them on deck. Five nuns had accompanied the kids, and two stood on the deck while the other three stayed in the boat.

Many of the visitors were little blonde kids the German army had left behind, and about four or five were little black kids. The guys who were carrying the kids up the ladder kept taking the white kids while the nuns tried to push the little black kids to them. The sailors kept pushing those kids away. Finally, when they got all the white kids aboard the white sailors refused to bring the black kids aboard. By now the nuns were hysterical and crying, and some were praying; the kids were crying too.

I was watching the whole thing. I ran to the officer on deck. He turned his back on me, so I went to the executive officer and told him what was going on. He looked indifferent, but he reluctantly went down to the quarterdeck and told the sailors to bring the kids aboard. I watched as they almost threw those kids on board. I heard

The USS *Shenandoah* in Venice, Italy about 1952

the word "nigger" several times. They sat all the black kids at tables away from the white kids and treated them like garbage.

It took me a long time to get over that. I was the senior black aboard the ship. I talked to the captain and some of the officers who were responsible. They all seemed to express, "What do you expect? Stay in your place and don't worry about something like this." Their actions were despicable, but typical.

The edge of that kind of thing was taken off when we visited a new port. I never got over the excitement of going someplace I had never been. We traveled up and down the shores of southern Europe, and there was a strong contrast when we went to North African countries like Morocco, Libya, Tunisia, and Egypt. My buddy and I saw all we could each time we hit a new port.

I'll never forget when we got lost in the Casbah in Morocco. The ship was to leave that evening, and we were hopelessly lost. None of the Arabs who lived there would talk to us. We got more and more desperate to find our way out. The place was like a maze. Finally we found the right way and got to the landing as the last boat was about to leave for the ship.

We went off the ship in Cyprus one day. We should have known better; there was a fierce war going on there. The communists were trying to take over the country. You could hear the gunfire day and night as the two factions fought each other. We were in this little town looking around at the beautiful view when all of a sudden a rifle bullet hit the ground between us; then another hit the wall by where we were standing. We slowly turned around and left. We knew that if the shooter had wanted to hit us, he would have. The guy was saying, "Get the hell away from here!"

In Libya one day my buddy and I were on liberty when we saw an Arab snake charmer who let us sit in front of his cobra and play his flute as the cobra weaved in front of us in the basket. I, like a fool, did it. There was a guy there with a camera who would take pictures and sell them to you for a price. The cobra was swaying in front of me about three feet away while I played the flute. I figured it out—the cobra could not strike out from the basket; it could only strike down and was unable to reach me as long as it was in the basket. Now that I look back on it I realize what a fool I was; I could have been wrong. I just wish I could find that picture.

It was shortly after World War II when we first went there; the Europeans ruled all of those countries then and the Arabs were treated like dogs. I had never seen people treated so badly; they had no rights. I saw Frenchmen kick them off the sidewalk because they didn't move soon enough. They wore Army blankets wrapped around them. Most of them had worn the blankets out—even the patches had patches—and there were sores all over their bodies.

When we sailors smoked a cigarette, there would be as many as a dozen people following us, waiting for us to throw the butt away. Then they would fight over it like a group of dogs after a bone; they were so anxious to get the butt so they could sell it and buy a little something to eat. They were not allowed in any of the public bars, restaurants, or anything like that. The few who had a house to live in were lucky. Many lived in small quarters about the size of one room. Some had a fence across the room so that they could keep the family goat or sheep inside lest someone steal it for food.

Returning to the States after one of those trips, our skipper, who was kind of flaky, decided he was going to set a record. So instead of going around a storm at sea, he decided to go through it. Normally the bow of the ship was about thirty-five feet above the water. In that storm the waves broke over the bow and slammed into the superstructure. The *Shenandoah* slid down into the space between the waves like a roller coaster, only to hit the next wall of water, which stopped her cold. The ship moaned and groaned as if she were in pain.

That fool, the captain, almost got us sunk; all the other officers aboard cursed him behind his back. We all prayed the ship could take it. The next day the sea smoothed out and the *Shenandoah* sailed along, seeming to tell the crew, "See what I can do?"

pieces 22

Back to California

We finally got back to Norfolk in spite of the fact that the captain had almost gotten us killed. Even though I was glad to get back to my wife and my two children—Karl was about three and Karen about a year old—I dreaded coming back to all the racial hate, discrimination, and insults.

One morning, a few days after my return, I was on my way to the ship on a bus. I was seated by the back door of the bus in my uniform. I noticed that the white driver kept looking at me in his rearview mirror. Finally he stopped, came all the way back to where I was sitting, and said to me, "Boy, I want you to take yo butt back there to the back of the bus."

I didn't even acknowledge him, I just continued to look out the window. After telling me one more time without a response, he got back behind the wheel and drove off, but he stopped at every intersection and looked both ways down the streets—seeking the police, I suppose.

I thought to myself, Here I have a wife and two small children. If he finds the police they will snatch me off the bus, take me to jail, and beat my butt, and probably fine me as well. I can't win. So I got up and moved the two or three rows to the back, where there were about six or more black folks sitting. They heaped their wrath upon me. "You ole folks from the North come down heah and make it hard for us," one said. "You should have did what that white man told you at first."

By the time I got to the ship I felt I was going to explode. I had

My children, Karen and Butch.

to do something. When the executive officer came to the wardroom for breakfast, I cornered him and asked if I could have a word with him. He could see I was upset, so he asked me to come to his office later. About ten o'clock or so I went to his office. When he saw me approach, he got up from his chair and asked if he could talk to me outside.

I explained to him how the race bigotry, hatred, and discrimination was getting to me. I indicated that I felt as though I was about to crack up, lose it, and just come apart at the seams. I asked him if he could send me back to California. The executive officer suggested and granted me a week off. Before the week was up the personnel officer aboard ship phoned and asked me to come to the office. I felt as though a ton had been lifted off my shoulders when they handed me papers reassigning me to two years of shore duty at Moffett Field in California—not that all the bigotry and prejudice was gone in California in 1953, but at least it was not the vicious hate I had experienced in the South.

The environment I moved to was not as stressful, and I felt I could handle it. My assignment to the Naval Air Station at Moffett Field was one of the most pleasant I had experienced in my Navy career. I had access to Oakland and San Francisco, which was only about a half hour away. I soon settled in and shortly thereafter purchased my home in Menlo Park. My two children were five and three years old; I now had about three and a half or four years before I could retire, so I looked forward to watching and helping them grow up. At the time I was one rank under chief petty officer, which was my goal to accomplish before I retired. I had various jobs at Moffett Field before taking a competitive examination, which included about six hundred other E-6 rated sailors hoping to make the new rate of chief petty officer. I finished close to the top of the pack and became chief in 1954. That was very gratifying to me because in those years there were few black members of the Navy who were chief petty officers, and very few who were commissioned officers. I was assigned to run the BOQ at Moffett Field. My job was to supervise, buy supplies, and create menus to feed about two hundred officers. The Korean War was in progress, and Moffett was the main base for officers coming and going to Korea. We took care of all the big shots. Our job was to be able to house and feed the people no matter what time they arrived; I had a special crew for that. To pat myself on the back a little, I did receive a commendation that stated our officers' mess was the best in the US Navy. All good things must come to an end, as they say, and eventually my time was up at Moffett Field. I managed to get my assignment extended for another six months, but that was the best they could do—now I had to go back to a ship. I was assigned to the USS *Oreskany*, an aircraft carrier where I was responsible for feeding and housing more than six hundred officers. That meant supervising one hundred and fifty men, buying supplies, and supervising the cooking, baking, and all the rest of over eighteen hundred meals per day. The officers who were pilots had certain dietary restrictions that had to be considered and integrated into the menu; sometimes I look back and wonder how I did it. I was on the assignment about a year, then received bad news: the *Oreskany* was being decommissioned, which meant I

Carl E. Clark washing his "Mach 1" Mustang, which he has been doing since 1971.

would be assigned to another ship. Through political maneuvering and some divine help, I was assigned to another ship close to home, the USS *Yorktown* of World War II fame. There my job was pretty much the same. I stayed aboard her until I retired from the Navy in 1958, after twenty-two years of service. I then landed a job in Menlo Park as a postman at the Menlo Park Post Office. I was my own mailman for about four years. I finally retired from the job in 1979, after twenty-one years of service.Since my retirement I have been living a life of leisure and doing all the things I always wanted to do.

Life can be good.

Carl E. Clark

Dad trying on the uniform he wore when he retired from the navy in 1958.

My father retired from the US Navy in 1958. He has been telling the stories of his life experiences to his family and friends for years. All of us have urged my father to write this book.

It is because of our persistent urging that he has given *Pieces from My Mind* for all to experience and enjoy.

The picture on this page is a recent photo of my father in the uniform he wore when he was in the Navy; it still fits, although he has much more gray hair than when he last wore it.

The time in which dad grew up and set out to experience life was a period of racial ugliness that ran deep in our country. This book merely reflects the overtones of those times. He does not personally harbor any racial animosities.

Karl "Butch" Clark, son